DYC

COLLEGII · D'YOUVILLE · SIGILLUM · SIGILLUM ·

RELIGIO ET SCIENTIA

MCMVIII

THE D'YOUVILLE FAMILY ALBUM:
ONE HUNDRED YEARS OF TEACHING AND CARING

David H. Kelly, PhD

THE
DONNING COMPANY
PUBLISHERS

THE D'YOUVILLE FAMILY ALBUM:

ONE HUNDRED YEARS OF TEACHING AND CARING

David H. Kelly, PhD

The Donning Company Publishers
184 Business Park Drive, Suite 206
Virginia Beach, VA 23462-6533

Steve Mull, General Manager and Project Director
Barbara Buchanan, Office Manager
Anne Cordray, Editor
Jennifer Peñaflor, Graphic Designer
Derek Eley, Imaging Artist
Tonya Hannink, Marketing Specialist
Susan Adams, Project Research Coordinator

Mary Taylor, Project Director

Library of Congress Cataloging-in-Publication Data

Kelly, David H.
        The D'Youville family album : one hundred years of teaching and caring / by David Kelly.
                p.   cm.
        Includes index.
        ISBN 978-1-57864-510-7 (hard cover : alk. paper)
1. D'Youville College—History. I. Title.
        LD1733.D88K45 2008
        378.747'97—dc22

2008028673

Printed in the United States of America by Walsworth Publishing Company

Table of Contents

Acknowledgments

There are many to thank, but like past D'Youville students, the first on the list are members of the Grey Nuns of the Sacred Heart. Sister R. Patricia Smith and Sister Mary Sheila Driscoll left valuable written records used throughout the work—both are well-remembered colleagues. Sister Mary Kathleen Duggan, the current archivist and past English professor, academic dean, and acting president of the college, has been incredibly generous with her time and knowledge and I thank her for reading the entire manuscript and making valuable additions throughout. Sister Mary Charlotte Barton helped with a very thoughtful interview, well used here, which helped me understand the transitions of the 1970s. Sister Denise Roche approved the entire project, the oral history seminar, granted a sabbatical, and literally gave me the keys to the archives. No one could have been more open. Like thousand of students from the past, staff members and faculty, working with these sisters and many others of the order has deeply enriched our lives.

In the interview process there are also many to thank. Wolodymir Babicky, Stephanie Balling, Jennifer Casali, Judith Dumitru, Jennifer Falbo, Clinton Gilliland, Keegan Harbajan, Lee Hellis, Edward Jurkiewicz, Elizabeth Lee, Scott Mueller, Nicholas Munding, Michael Nolan, Elizabeth Reeves, Christopher Reda, Nicholas Richter, Edem Tsiagbey, and Brian Walzak took the class in oral history that did many of the interviews. Brian Jones interviewed his grandmother and her friends who attended in the 1930s and synthesized the material in a senior thesis. Steve Bennett, a graduating senior, helped as a volunteer on several occasions. While all the interviews are the basis of the study, those with Joseph Grande and Robert Murphy (along with those of the two presidents) added enormously to my understanding of D'Youville.

Thanks also to Tom Milano who spend hours trying to follow questionable instructions to prepare the photos to be sent off in some reasonable order.

Finally, I wish to thank my wife, Ruth Kelly, for not being too bored when I talked about the research at numerable social occasions, but as a wonderful storyteller who appears in these pages, and who, as an alumna and colleague, read the entire manuscript to point out questionable areas and historical foibles.

Prologue

By 1847 the Diocese of Buffalo, New York, with Bishop John Timon at its head, had sixteen churches properly staffed with priests. Timon worked carefully and came from Irish and German (half of whom were Catholic) immigrants. By 1860 Buffalo was America's tenth largest city. Timon responded to both the growth and the divisions within the Catholic community. He realized he needed help and actively recruited religious orders to come to Buffalo. In 1848 he brought the Sisters of Charity who created Buffalo's first hospital. (Buffalo General Hospital, the Protestant answer, was founded a decade later in 1858.)[1] Timon responded to a public school movement in the 1850s by launching thirty-seven Catholic elementary schools while he was in office.[2] Timon faced a division in the Catholic community with the strength of the German groups (almost half the city population and builders of the first great cathedral—Saint Louis Cathedral) and the growth of the Irish element. (By the 1920s Poles would be a quarter of the Buffalo population and Italians would be the third largest ethnic group.) The German laity struggled with Timon over possession of Saint Louis Cathedral and Timon answered with the building of a new cathedral (Saint Joseph's) standing sharply above Buffalo's waterfront.[3]

But Timon also sought to diffuse the division—one method was to recruit broad help in Europe. In 1849 he invited the Oblates of Mary Immaculate to found a parish in Buffalo. The Oblates were a recent French order founded by Father de Mazenod in 1816 to revive Catholicism in the South of France after the French Revolution. The Oblates were a missionary order. They already had missions to Canada and the United States (which was officially viewed as an area of missionary endeavor throughout the nineteenth century). The Oblates arrived in Buffalo in 1851 and purchased eighteen acres of land bounded by Porter, Plymouth, Connecticut, and Fargo Avenues (site of Buffalo's first Alms house). The first church opened

John Timon, first bishop of Buffalo. From 1847 to 1867, the revered Bishop Timon helped organize institutions to meet the growing needs of the Catholic immigrant population of the city.

Eugene de Mazenod, bishop of Marseilles, France. Born in 1782 his noble family fled France for Italy during the French Revolution. When he returned to Napoleonic France in 1802 he became a priest—going from village to village to re-awaken Catholic values. In 1826 he and his followers created the Oblates of Mary Immaculate. This missionary order worked in Canada and was invited to Buffalo by Bishop Timon. Bishop de Mazenod was recognized as a saint in 1995.

Marguerite D'Youville, foundress of the Grey Nuns of Montreal. Born in 1701 and widowed with six children in 1729, she ran a general store to support two surviving sons and to pay off her husband's debts. Called to charity she took in the poor and attracted other women to help her. The government of Montreal asked her to take over the general hospital, which was in collapse. With hard work, sewing for self-support, these sisters dedicated all to charity and expanded the range of the hospital. She died in 1771 and the Church venerated her in the 1890s and recognized her as a saint in 1990. The college would be named for her.

in 1852 and the present Holy Angels Church was begun in 1856. The Oblates proceeded to build not only a church, but an educational complex. By 1857 they, with the help of the Grey Nuns (Sisters of Charity of Ottawa), opened an elementary school in the old Alms house of the property they'd purchased. By 1880 a large school building was erected along West Avenue; in 1891 the Holy Angels Collegiate Institute (a junior seminary for men) was placed beside the church on Porter Avenue.[4]

The Oblates had a firm connection with the Grey Nuns initially from Montreal. In 1844 the Oblates called on the Grey Nuns to work with them in the Red River area of Canada (Manitoba) with French Canadian and Meti (mixed French and Native American) populations. This work involved education as well as care for the poor. The Grey Nuns of Montreal had experimented with education but questioned adding it to their mission. A year later, again called by the Oblates, four Grey Nuns traveled to Bytown (Ottawa) to establish a house both for education and care of the poor. One of these sisters, Elizabeth Bruyere (only twenty-seven) became the leader due to the illness of an older sister. Their first act, four days after arrival, was to begin teaching—Sister Bruyere in French and Sister Rodriques (Ellen Howard, an Irish immigrant who had joined the order four years earlier) in English. Some of this rush was a response to a Protestant drive for education in Bytown. At first, the authorities found the sisters' teaching to be acceptable, but second rate. Sister Bruyere admonished her fellow sisters to devote time to study and improvement and brought them to a higher level. While the sisters continued their commitment to care of the poor their focus grew on education. Indeed, the local bishop in Bytown officially added "ou a l'instruction des jeune filles (the instruction of young ladies)" to their official charge. The bishop's broadening of the sisters' work required charging tuition to fund the schools, while the nuns in Montreal were not allowed to charge for their charitable work. Such differences led both groups to agree that the Bytown group (and all such daughter communities) must have freedom to follow local rule.[5] When Father Edward Chevalier, OMI, was sent from Ottawa to Buffalo by the ecclesiastical center in France, he had worked with the Grey Nuns of the Cross in Ottawa and invited them to aid him in Buffalo.

Mother Elizabeth Bruyere. In 1845 Sister Bruyere became the leader of the Grey Nuns in Ottawa, at twenty-seven (an older sister had died). While continuing charitable work they established schools for girls. She insisted on advanced teaching skills. She accompanied the initial sisters to Buffalo in 1857. In 1873 she noted about the Grey Nuns in Buffalo as they began building the new Holy Angels Academy building, "This Buffalo House, our first mission has caused me more worry than the others. It appears to be the most backward, but for all that, it will end by being the most important of all our houses." [6]

Holy Angels Parish, the destiny of Father Chevalier (and eventually the Grey Nuns), was at the northern border of Buffalo, near to where it merged with the separate village of Black Rock. The Erie Canal was connected to Lake Erie and terminated a mile and a half to the south of the parish. Much of the land to the south of the parish was the large estate of Mr. Fargo (of the Wells-Fargo Express Company). The estate had middle-class housing near it and in 1900 would be broken up into more middle-class housing. The area to the north and east of the parish (to the west was the canal, the river, and for a time the water reservoir of the city) was lower middle-class and skilled workers' housing in which no ethnic group predominated. The lower middle-class came as migrants from the rural areas; the skilled workers plied their skills maintaining the boats on the canal and were of German and Irish ethnic stock. The Irish who lived in South Buffalo did the physical labor of transferring grain and tended to be poorer since there was a distinct seasonal aspect to their labor. Another middle-class touch to the immediate neighborhood was the Pierce Hotel. Dr. Pierce had built this elaborate edifice as a supplement to his mail-order medicine business (folks could come for a cure). The hotel burned to the ground in 1881. As a parish Holy Angels consisted of skilled workers and some clerks located on the borders of middle-class and working-class neighborhoods.[7]

Pierce Hotel. This huge Victorian edifice was raised by Dr. Pierce to treat patients through the rest cure and the continued use of his patent medicine. It helped define the character of Holy Angels Parish, virtually around the corner from the church and now part of the campus. It burned to the ground in 1881.

Laboratory at Holy Angels Academy in 1893. The apparatus and look is very similar to that at the leading women's colleges for the teaching of science.

In October 1857, Mother Bruyere accompanied five sisters, Mother Saint Peter, Sister Saint Augustine, Sister Kelly, Sister Saint Mary Patrick, and Sister Raisinne who traveled to Toronto and then to Buffalo. The parishioners were not ready for them, but soon a house was found on Plymouth Street for their residence—a walk over plank sidewalks to the church and school. Classes began in the parish school on November 4. The school was located in a building of the old poor house at the center of the Holy Angels land; it had fifteen boys and eleven girls as pupils, all "very unruly." The sisters also faced a harsh Buffalo winter and local women helped them sew cloaks in bright red calico (someone donated the fabric). The cloaks were so heavily quilted that they could stand on edge by themselves. They fit loosely over the sisters' gray habits. These warm cloaks helped the sisters survive (Mother Bruyere was in despair when she left to return to Ottawa). They survived not only the walk to work, but the sisters also began charitable work in the community through visits to the sick and the imprisoned.[8]

In 1861 Bishop Timon urged the Grey Nuns to enlarge their efforts (as in his original request) and begin a select academy for young ladies. Despite some trepidation from the local parish, afraid they might lose their elementary school, the sisters found a house on Niagara Street that was suitable and Holy Angels Academy opened with twelve students. By January there were thirty-six students (including eight Protestants) registered at all levels, elementary to advanced. The curriculum included language, drawing, water color, and harp lessons. (Both at Holy Angels and the earlier Nardin Academy, the proper teaching of French was an attraction to the elite of Buffalo. These schools depended on tuition and were not subsidized.) "Sister Olier taught us French in those days. A tiny, little nun she was, with too much brain for her frail body; a brilliant, charming

Library of Holy Angels Academy in 1893. Note the relative scarcity of books, the comfort of the room, and the wide use of religious symbolism.

Architectural drawing in 1901 for the expansion of Holy Angels Academy that inspired Bishop Colton to think about a college for women.

personality, reminding one somewhat of the famous women of the French salons."[9] By 1861 the academy (Grey Nuns continued to serve the parish school as well) had succeeded to the degree it needed more space. The sisters attempted to borrow money and buy a more extensive property. The motherhouse in Ottawa disallowed this action for several years. In 1871 the Grey Nuns in Buffalo received permission to borrow from Ottawa, but also incorporating as the Grey Nuns under New York State law. They purchased land opposite of Holy Angels Church for $18,000, using $3,000 in cash and the second Niagara Street property.

At the urging of Bishop Ryan they began building (although initial attempts to borrow money failed). In 1872 they did get a bank loan and in 1874 the new building opened.[10] In 1879 fire destroyed much of this building. "It is tradition that Sister Saint Bridget remained in the convent [the school and convent were one]…walking up and down the lower corridor, reciting her rosary, and insisting the convent would not, could not burn." (The firemen ultimately put her out as they fought the fire.)[11] The fire, although devastating, stirred sympathy of the surrounding community. The Oblates donated space for temporary classes. The Grey Nuns rebuilt the academy with some skimping because they lacked full fire insurance.

The academy grew through the 1880s and 1890s as did the Grey Nuns' educational work in Buffalo and New York State. Three local schools had Grey Nun teachers, and others traveled to Medina, Ogdensburg, and Plattsburg.[12] By the 1890s Holy Angels Academy was recognized as a leading school for women in the state. Students reached the regents level by their third year and yet spent another to complete the course. Pictures sent to a display at the Columbian Exhibition in Chicago in 1893 showed up-to-date laboratories, etc. The Grey Nun faculty also shepherded some students to the exhibition. The academy was staffed mainly by sisters, the quality of their work guaranteed by the rules laid down by Mother Bruyere that all teaching members meet the French Normal School standard. Indeed, the training at Holy Angels Academy qualified its graduates to teach in primary grades.[13]

In 1901 someone reported to the building inspector that the upper floors of the academy were too weak. He banned large assemblies in the main hall on the third floor. The sisters, already in need of space, began planning to add two large wings to the original building (which had been slightly expanded in 1887 and 1899) and to strengthen the building. When the sketch of this proposed building was published in the *Illustrated Buffalo Express* it inspired in Bishop Charles Colton of Buffalo a grander vision.

By that date, constantly urged on by the bishops, the Oblates and the Grey Nuns had created a viable parish with an elementary school. The Oblates had added a minor seminary, which would shortly (1902) become a day school or more general secondary school for boys. The Grey Nuns taught in the parish school and had founded a more elite academy (which operated at elementary and secondary levels). Some graduates of the academy did join the Grey Nuns and the order staffed other parish schools. Bishop Colton saw a growing educational complex in northwest Buffalo and envisioned a college for women.

¹ David Gerber, *The Making of American Pluralism: Buffalo, New York, 1825-1860*. Urbana: University of Illinois Press, 1989, p. 6.

² Joseph Grande and Scott Eberle, *Second Looks; A Pictorial History of Buffalo and Erie County*, Norfolk: Donning, 1987, p. 60, 62, 74.

³ Ibid. 71; Gerber, p. 280-317.

⁴ Robert Chambers, ed. *Holy Angels Church, 1851-2002*.

⁵ Sister R. Patricia Smith, GNSH, "Grey Nuns: Educational Work in Western NY," typescript, p. 2-5, D'Youville College archives. Comment by Sister Mary Kathleen Duggan, D'Youville Archivist.

⁶ Sister R. Patricia Smith, p. 13.

⁷ Eberle and Grande, p. 42, 59. Gerber, p. 17. Eberle and Grande, p. 42, 59. Gerber, p. 17.

⁸ Sister R. Patricia Smith, p. 9-10; Elizabeth Cronin, "A Retrospective," *D'Youville Magazine*, Vol. 1, No. 1 (November 1908) p. 6. Sister Mary Sheila Driscoll, "The Beginning of the Grey Nuns in Buffalo," typescript, 1968.

⁹ Cronin, p. 9.

¹⁰ Sister R. Patricia Smith, p. 12. Sister Mary Sheila Driscoll, p. 12.

¹¹ Crinon, p. ll.

¹² Sister R. Patricia Smith, p. 13

¹³ Sister Mary Kathleen Duggan. "On the Spirit of the Place," *D'Mensions* (Spring 2006), p. 15; Sister R. Patricia Smith, p. 13-14.

Chapter One

From Founding to War's End

When Bishop Charles Colton suggested upgrading the academy to a college, he found trepidation and support. Reasons for trepidation could be found simply by looking at the other Catholic college in Buffalo — Canisius. German Jesuits built Canisius on the German pro-gymnasium model and it was primarily a secondary school. Both Bishop John Timon and later Bishop Stephen V. Ryan had pushed for a college component using the traditional nine-year Jesuit course, teaching the classics as the core of curriculum. In 1884, the Jesuits split the school into a secondary school and a college. The secondary school had 248 students by 1905, but the college had a mere 23 students in 1884 and just 19 in 1903.[1]

Bishop Colton did find supporters and sound reasons to push forward. Among the Grey Nuns, a major advocate was Sister Saint Stanislaus who argued for the college. She served as its first president from 1908-1911 and again from 1913-1916, after a break to recover from illness. Father Nelson Baker from Lackawanna also strongly supported the idea. Father Baker was an inspirational leader who took his steel-working, grain-loading parishioners into an institution building spree with a home for boys, a foundling hospital, a regular hospital, and eventually the most glorious church in the Buffalo area — Our Lady of Victory — modeled after *Sacre-Coeur* in Paris. Father Baker had helped the Grey Nuns obtain the bank loan to add the Prospect wing in 1907.[2]

Physically laying the foundation of the college.

15

These supporters reflected the optimism of their community. The Buffalo population was reaching a half million. Immigration brought tens of thousands of Polish to the city.[3] These immigrants needed priests and teachers (sisters, brothers, or laity) who supported Catholicism. Small numbers at Canisius College might have been disappointing, but no college in the United States was very large; the average (median) private institution only had 128 students in 1897 – only 359 by 1924. Because state institutions existed that had more students, the average (again median) student attended a larger institution, but still the average college had only 505 students in 1897. Women were definitely part of the growth of more advanced education. When Holy Angels Academy came into existence, there were six thousand female seminaries or academies. Some of these, like the Bryn Mawr School in Baltimore, had rigorous curriculum – teaching Latin and Greek – to produce women capable of entering elite women's colleges. (Holy Angels Academy curriculum was in this rigorous tradition.) Several of these academies – the most prominent being Mount Holyoke – had made the transition from academy to college. Women also were attending co-ed colleges and universities – by 1900, 71% of the 85,000 women enrolled in college were at such co-ed institutions. Indeed women outnumbered men at the University of Michigan in 1900. Bishops across America, including Buffalo's Bishop Colton, reacted. By World War I, Catholics had opened ten colleges for women – D'Youville College among them as the second Catholic women's college in New York State and the first women's college of any sort in western New York. D'Youville was the second institution in Buffalo to grant the bachelor of arts degree; the first was Canisius College. (The University of Buffalo, founded in 1846, only granted law and medical degrees.)[4]

16

Notice the building does not conform to the architect's rendering shown in the Prologue—the older gothic wing remains as it does to this day.

D'YOUVILLE COLLEGE, BUFFALO, NEW YORK

The entire student body in 1912 posed on the steps of the original building.
Note the prevalence of the almost formal white frock.

Bishop Colton might have envisioned the expansion and the need was apparent, but the Grey Nuns had to make it happen. Sister Saint Stanislaus led the effort to create the college. Sisters recruited from the academy went to Ottawa for a Normal School Certificate and to summer programs at Catholic University of America. Sister Mary Agnes, who would be the first dean of the college, went to Vassar to examine curriculum.[5]

The college taught a curriculum that reflected its academy past. Students took seventy-five points in courses (a point was equivalent to two hours of in-class teaching). The college mandated four points in religion, four points in church history (non-Catholics could take extra electives in this area), eleven points in philosophy, eight points in Latin, ten points in English, four points in history, six points in modern language, six points in science, four points in mathematics, and eighteen points in electives (in the junior and senior year, two of these elective points could be in pedagogy). The concentration in Latin, philosophy, and religion demonstrated the traditional nature of the curriculum. The college offered electives in business but most electives were in art and music, reflecting the strength of the academy.[6] By the 1890s, this sort of curriculum generated some controversy as being outdated. Some women's colleges tried to subordinate their past lives as academies by focusing on more science.[7]

Charles Eliot, the president of Harvard University, raised questions about the rigidity of a curriculum oriented toward classics. Harvard refused to accept transfers of credit from most Jesuit colleges (with some exception made for Georgetown University) because the curriculum was too classical.[8]

CATHOLICS felt it was they who could bring culture to CRUDE AMERICA. Throughout the late nineteenth century, the major journal of the Catholic community, *The Catholic World*, PREACHED this message.

Women couldn't get into Harvard University in any case and the founder of D'Youville College thought Catholic traditions were superior. Nor did they wish to toss away the strengths of their academy foundation. To strengthen enrollment and in the spirit of this conservative curriculum, the college began an extension program for teachers primarily in languages in 1915, and then in 1916 an extensive summer program was added with four English courses, six Latin courses, eight modern foreign language classes, two education classes, and a number of other individual courses.[9] The institution moved classes to late afternoon to accommodate the program and obviously to serve women already teaching.[10] In 1915, an advertisement in the *D'Youville Magazine* portrayed a school of painting and design. In 1916, the state of New York approved the addition of a bachelor of arts in music at the college and two years later the state approved a new two-year program to prepare school music supervisors.[11] The summer school history program listed for 1919 consisted of one course on the current war, two in American History, and one from a breakdown of European History into medieval, early modern, and modern areas. The curriculum denoted by this breakdown was typical of colleges across the country.[12]

In 1918-19, the *D'Youville Magazine* listed the faculty. Of twenty-five faculty members, three had some form of doctorate (in literature, religion, and music), four more had masters of art degrees. These ratios compared well to leading women's colleges in the 1890s where one eighth to one quarter of the faculty had doctorates. Of the faculty, there were nine lay men, one priest, three lay women, and twelve sisters. Noting that some faculty taught more than a single subject – nine faculty taught music (about one third the whole faculty); six faculty taught modern language, and three faculty taught classical language (another third of the whole). There were two teaching history, three faculty taught science and/or mathematics, three faculty taught English, and the priest taught logic and psychology. Even without counting the sisters, the gender ratio in the faculty was 20% women (in 1900 only 6.4% of academics were women). With the sisters there were fifteen women and ten men, or a 60% ratio. Sixty percent is far better than the peak of female academic employment in 1930 at 32.5%, but obviously less than a college like Smith which was almost entirely staffed by women.[13]

If the D'Youville curriculum seemed a bit traditional, perhaps the reason lay in the justification for founding the college. Higher education for women began in the seminary movement using the idea that educated mothers would raise better, more republican sons; or sons who would maintain some particular religious faith. This was a particularly strong motive in the Quaker academies. This argument of preparing for motherhood didn't disappear as the level of education moved from secondary

The first graduates, Pauline Garnett (seated) in history, Mary Brennan (right) in Latin, and Elizabeth Gosselin in French. Notice the spray of roses later to be incorporated in the alma mater.

to tertiary. Charlotte Meagher argued in this vein in the first issue of the *D'Youville Magazine*. She also referred to the impact of other previously educated women – Sister Hilda, Saint Bridgit, Saint Therese, and George Sand.[14]

As the nineteenth century progressed, educating women went beyond motherhood and shifted to preparation for professions. The key profession was teaching. From one fifth to one quarter of white New England women taught school at some point in their lives. The needs of education were obvious in booming Buffalo and among Catholics in the city. Many of D'Youville College's early programs aimed specifically at providing and enhancing teacher skills. Better skills were in demand throughout the area and nationally. Progressive reform movements focused on the schools at precisely the time when D'Youville College was founded.[15]

While preparing women to be mothers or to enter teaching lay in the background of D'Youville College's origins, the founders had another core concept in mind. Catholics felt it was they who could bring culture to crude America. Throughout the late nineteenth century, the major journal of the Catholic community, *The Catholic World*, preached this message. At D'Youville College's first commencement (1912), Director of Studies William A. Martin, professor of English and Philosophy and holder of a master's degree, argued that the goal of the college was to educate better women, ones who could fully express spiritual and other forces of the heart; who would know how to ascertain the truth and who would develop sobriety, restraint, and humility (like that of Socrates). Martin claimed the college's goal was to keep the "poet alive" and improve "the cultural experience of the race." If men wanted cooks and sewers, they could go to the employment office.[16]

In the first issue of the *D'Youville Magazine*, Mary O'Connor wrote that "men who opposed women's education were stodgy old professors, the second-rate thinkers, and some impoverished chaps who only have their gender to provide a sense of superiority." She also ended on the cultural theme, but a bit more succinctly, "an educated soul has more capacity for enjoyment." A few years later, another student took on more educated company criticizing the notion in Shakespeare, Thackery, and Hardy that smart and clever women are necessarily bad – she rather liked Becky Sharp.[17]

This emphasis on culture might strike one as elitist. Going to college certainly was a mark of the elite in the early twentieth century – indeed, any education beyond eighth grade might be so considered. Tuition at D'Youville was $100 per year. While this compared favorably to the tuition at Vassar College which was $300 per year, the total cost at D'Youville College – board and tuition – was $400, and a room added from $50 to $150 (fees at the academy were just $50 less). In 1910, the average wage in industrial occupations was $630 per year. These fees were expensive. The middle class nature of D'Youville students also was sensed by advertisers in the *D'Youville Magazine* with all major department stores placing an ad – in the fourth issue of the third volume, three piano dealers advertised.[18]

The cultural theme evident in defending the founding of the college continued as part of the spirit of the college. The nine young ladies who were the original student body had the audacity to begin the *D'Youville Magazine* in their first year and it was continued for five decades. The magazine came out quarterly and was about seventy pages per issue. It occasionally included material from other places,

20

Some of the resident students in a less formal picture from 1910-1911.

but usually students wrote, or at least translated the articles. The editors meant the magazine to be of general interest to the public of Buffalo and they took part in presenting and defending Catholic culture. Fourteen of the thirty articles in the first volume related to such themes – saints' lives, culture from Catholic Europe, praise of medieval civilization. For each volume in the entire decade, Catholic culture remained a theme with about seven articles on average appearing per volume.

The students also presented creative writing – short stories and poems. In the third volume they began to present critical essays which seem to be papers prepared for classes that were improved for publication. The magazine was a guide to the editors' and writers' mentality, the curriculum of the school, student opinion – in editorials. The magazine also reported on school activities. In all it served as a guide to student life.

Over the decade, the most common entry in the *D'Youville Magazine* was the sentimental short story (these averaged ten per volume). These stories were supplemented with another one or two sentimental tales with a distinctively religious theme – like re-conversion to Catholicism in death, or a good man from Boston converting a New England town by his example of devotion. Many of the stories were about courtship or family life. Stories about the past were often placed in the medieval period. One, set earlier in ancient Sparta, depicted a mother who refused to expose her weakling son and was exiled with him. Similar to these sentimental stories were twenty additional works that dealt with fantasy or science fiction (for example, fallen stars being the origin of starfish). Realist stories did appear, but only one third to one quarter as often as the sentimental tale. These young women were romantics. Even the realist stories often dealt with young married folks or child care. Oddly, only four stories of college life were printed – two of these reflected a young man from a rural area going off to college and becoming a football hero – i.e. they had nothing to do with the D'Youville College experience. Often these stories, whether sentimental or realist, aimed at an ironic ending – clearly O'Henry was the model short story writer for these young women. The poetry they produced included

Portrait of Mary Garnett in her graduation robes in 1913. Mary was an early editor of the D'Youville Magazine. She went on to earn an MA and then tragically died shortly after. ——

Cover from the third year of the D'Youville Magazine. *Notice the stylized corn and the general appearance which echoes that of the arts and crafts movement organized by Elwood Hubbard just outside of Buffalo in East Aurora.* ——————————

religious imagery and themes, but far more often was secular – depicting nature, the change of seasons, fairies at sunset. A minor chord about death appears in several.

These sentimental young women generally rejected the political reform of the day. One editorial took on settlement houses – partially on a Social Darwinist basis that charity hinders the poor, partially on the idea that the houses denigrate immigrant (i.e. Catholic) culture. It concluded with support for Catholic charity. They opposed free lunches in public schools. (One editorial did support playgrounds for children.) Another attacked Teddy Roosevelt and another dismissed politicians as ward healers. In 1919 there appeared a vicious attack on strikes as anarchist sickness.[19] One of the great reforms they lived through was the demand for the women's vote. The suffragette movement was attacked in editorials in 1909, in 1912, and even after the reform was a reality in 1918. An article in 1909 saw women as having the full range of opportunity. An article in 1916 also saw no value in the work of Ibsen. This anti-feminism was broken only once in the article noted above that protested that strong women in literature were often seen as evil.[20]

While the students rejected contemporary forms of feminism, they identified with women's roles as cultural arbiters and mothers who raised cultured sons and daughters. In the magazine they defended the arts, from elocution and the art of conversation, to the need for music in the schools, and the value of the visual arts. Editorials attacked too many fairytales, adults attending movies and bad theater. They ran dozens of articles on art or music and many items classified as Catholic culture (the religious painting of Murillo) were in that context.

The college offered speakers that urged this view on the students – from a commencement address by the poet Joyce Kilmer, to a later lecture (after he was killed in World War I) by his widow, and public lectures by Dr. Henry Lappin, an esteemed early professor and member of the Royal Society of Literature.[21]

23

These young women who supported culture and were not enamored with women's votes also found their parents less than stodgy. An editorial disputed the concept that a college girl was alien to her parents' life. In a story about two parents and a young lady, all inviting a potential suitor to the house (the father wanted a man's man, the mother someone cultured, the daughter's view was less defined), all three invited the same young gentleman. Another story attempted to fool a father into accepting a young man by a canoe rescue but clearly the father was not fooled, but went along anyway. Studies at other colleges have shown such agreement between mothers and daughters, at least, was common in the era.[22]

The young women also expressed conservative (or romantic) attitudes toward philosophy and science. In the first volume an editorial attacked but clearly understood the relativism of William James. Later editorials defended scholasticism as proper philosophy, but also the value of studying logic. One editorial even praised dogma. Another editorial attacked learning math, but this seemed the typical complaint of an English major who disliked numbers.[23] In science, Darwin's ideas were attacked in the first volume and then at the centenary of his birth twice more. These editorials did not object to his theory being taught or even say it was wrong. Rather they saw evolution as incomplete – missing the beauty of creation. The later editorial preferred an emotional response to the beauty of nature rather than its analysis. While they preferred the romance of literature they were not completely anti-science. One long article defended the need for animal experimentation and another (in World War I) advocated essentially creating an American chemical and dye-stuff industry.[24]

24

D'Youville students in 1917 being a little less formal with the lake in the backdrop and the sailor suit becoming a motif. —————

Students from 1913 to 1919 demonstrating a personal intimacy that kept these students loyal to one another and to the college over time. Close female contact and friendship reflected nineteenth century standards.

The young women were middle-class or wished to be. Some of them had traveled. The journal had a description of the ruins of Saint Andrews, the Alhambra, letters from travels in Spain, and later in the decade one student author described voyaging through the Philippines, the Dutch East Indies (Indonesia), and to Japan. The settings of the stories they wrote were usually lush – the princess in the castle, the southern manor house before or during the Civil War, the family gathered at the ancestral home or the extensive summer house, elite men's clubs, etc. They described long-term visits of relatives, debutante parties, and summer outings at grand resorts. When they described slums, those slums were in foreign cities or in parts of the city far from their lives. These stories do not have the authenticity of Edith Wharton, but seem more like the young ladies wanted to be there but had not quite arrived. They did express resentment at the Protestant upper classes with attack on the prestige of ancestors on the *Mayflower* or being members of the Daughters of the American Revolution (DAR).[25]

Occasionally political issues that echoed in the Catholic press reached the pages of the magazine. For example

25

Mirabelle Berst in 1919 in her Joan of Arc costume for the traditional spring play. These plays were a highlight of the school year.

one editorial approved of the execution of a Spanish anarchist. Such commentary most often related to Ireland. Several stories appeared in the regular journal with Irish mythical or nationalist themes. The Irish poet, Padraic Colum, spoke at the college. This event was reported and a poem and short story by him were included. Editorials chastised the English for the history of the famine, argued that home rule for Ireland was a necessity. In 1916, after the repression of the Easter Uprising, those executed were called martyrs. A year later, the editor published a fervent Irish nationalist manifesto later attributed to Sister Saint Stanislaus Burns, president of the college.[26]

The most intense political issue faced by these young women was, of course, World War I, which tore apart Europe, but only slowly affected America. The initial comment on the war appeared in the reprint in 1915 of a speech by Nan O'Reilly, at a joint college meeting to celebrate one hundred years of peace between Britain and the U.S. The speech defends the Catholic idea of just war (but labels neither antagonist) and then goes on to argue women need to educate men to avoid war. There also was a rare piece on German literature, Gerhardt Hauptman, in the issue as if to balance any pro-English bias. A few issues later, articles appeared on the war poetry of Brook and Kilmer, both of which praised the heroism of war. By the last issue of 1914-15, an article again by Nan O'Reilly took a Canadian perspective and essentially accused a young objector to the war of slacking. Generally, the romantic view of war prevailed, with several comments on slackers and women's war work after America entered the war. In 1916, the real war did enter the pages in stories of, again, a Canadian young man who goes off to war, only to have his girlfriend forget him, and another where all the soldiers in the tale are killed. Only in 1920 did a faculty member give a speech that truly criticized the war.[27]

The students' response to the D'Youville curriculum was reflected in the magazine. Their response was tempered by gender and a relatively conservative and Catholic content. There appeared articles on Marie Antoinette, Maria Theresa, a lady in waiting to Empress Josephine, Italian women in the Renaissance, Mary Stewart, Madam deStael, as well as women saints. The editors mixed an interest with women into their historical essays. This fascination also appeared in some sixteen articles that reflected classical literature study. While they wrote general themes on Greek literature or Roman plays, they also researched the dress of both Greek and Roman women and paid careful attention to the use of makeup, particularly mascara among Roman women.

26

The editors of the magazine were literature majors. Pieces did appear on history and culture, some eleven on music for example. But literature was their passion. They published, over the twelve years, ninety-four articles on various authors and literary forms. Within the ninety-four, their favored author was Shakespeare. Often they wrote of female characters or of art and music within Shakespeare. With English literature (by far the most common subject) the next favored authors were Dickens (three articles), Chaucer (four), and Milton. The only modern British writer they admired was Joseph Conrad with several articles, and three laudatory items on Rupert Brook (Belloc and Chesterton were praised and reviewed). Aside from these traditional and Catholic writers, the romantic school from England, Europe, and America (Poe) received attention. They wrote seven articles over the twelve years on English romantics, five on European romantics, and one on America. Their interest in gender appeared in articles on Ophelia and an attack on the misogyny of Moliere.

They tended to ignore American literature; only ten articles appeared. Their favored authors were Robert Frost and Booth Tarkington (the latter is not really enshrined in the current literary canon, but was fairly popular at the turn of the century).[28]

They did not like realism, the primary literary movement in America in this decade. They specifically attacked the idea in the European novels of Zola. They thought Twain was too vulgar to read and even poor John Mansfield (poet laureate of England) came under criticism for using street idiom – again too vulgar. They thought free verse was abominable and that modernism had no basis for existence. The real future of literature lay with the ideas of Maeterlinck and the creation of new fairytales.[29]

The writers the editors praised were often Catholic, often women, and very obscure – none reached the contemporary literary canon. They included the novelist George Meredith, poets Anne Sedgewick, Alice Meynell, Ralph Hodgson, Rosamond Marriot Watson, and Padraic Colum (who spoke at the college). Kilmer has not been indicated in the list because one poem, "Trees," is well loved. Generally, they believed poetry should rhyme, be in proper language, and present a loving, graceful picture.

If their literary taste was toward the proper, so was their musical activity. The college arranged rich musical programs. In 1908, Alice Forting of Boston gave a piano concert – she was the major student of Carl Faelton (whose system of instruction was used at the college). The next year the faculty arranged a six-concert chamber music series. In 1910, faculty member Anthony Stenkowitch performed a piano concert from Grieg to Bach. In 1914, a concert of the contemporary composer MacDowell was performed. These were some of the special programs at the college – by 1912 there were two separate music societies and every spring they gave rich concert presentations. By 1914, the college also took the students to off-campus performances of the Boston, Minneapolis, Cincinnati, and Philadelphia orchestras – the last under the baton of the legendary conductor Fritz Kreisler.[30]

The college also sponsored single lectures and lecture series to broaden the curriculum. The speakers were highly respected, usually Catholic. Focusing on the students as women, the college presented Mrs. Thomas Carpenter for several lectures in household chemistry (an early version of home economics). This noncredit lecture series was repeated for several years. The college also offered in 1909 lectures

27

Classes were small in
THE FIRST DECADE,
starting with only six
and having **NINETEEN
GRADUATES** in 1919.

by Mrs. Jon W. Carroll, MD, on physiology and nutrition (such lectures were common at women's colleges, sometimes leading to credit courses and science departments which they did not at D'Youville). Individual lectures were given by visiting scholars from Catholic University, Fordham University, and Columbia University. The presidents of Niagara University and Canisius College both gave lectures at different times. Usually these lectures were on philosophy or literature; occasionally they were of more practical content, as Mrs. McCoskey of Brooklyn warned the students of the dangers of intermarriage.[31]

The biggest official celebration of the year was opening day when the bishop came to say Mass – and usually gave the rest of the day off. Opening day of 1911 saw the bishop accompanied by six priests (three taught at the college) at Mass. The second big celebration after 1912 was graduation. In 1912, for the first graduation, Cardinal Farley said Mass. He was accompanied by Bishop Colton, the bishops of Rochester and Ogdensberg, and five other priests including Father Baker and a representative of the Oblates. Dean Sister Mary Agnes drew the wildest cheers and Mother Kirby came from Ottawa with Sister Stanislaus, the former president. The students performed a musical evening under Ms. Cronyn (who received an honorary doctorate) and the tradition of a senior play, *As You Like It*, began. The banquet capped off several days of celebration. The banquets and senior play continued through the decade. Eventually, the banquets became an event where students honored faculty. The plays for the first few years were Shakespeare – *A Midsummer Night's Dream* and *The Tempest*, but by 1917 it was *Aladdin and His Wonderful Lamp*.[32]

The college did not control all student activities. With approval students managed *D'Youville Magazine*, had two musical societies, and prepared plays. They also debated and then organized sororities – Alpha Sigma, Kappa Chi, and Sodality of Children of Mary. Since two sororities existed and the student body was very small, everyone was included. Nor were there separate quarters for sororities, etc. The students also organized French and German clubs, a literary society, a current events club, and during World War I, a Red Cross Workers Organization. By 1918, the Student Government and Student Council were operating.[33]

The students and the college made holidays days of fun and celebration. The first was Halloween when various combinations of classes entertained their fellow students with a party – some of which was a modest initiation of freshmen to the college. Saint Valentine's Day also was a time for parties. Later in the decade, the Irish heritage of many of the students came to the forefront when Saint Patrick's Day became the day to celebrate alumnae of both Holy Angels Academy and the college. The college students put on a tea for the graduating seniors of the academy (and urged them to join the college side).[34]

These formal activities revolved around food, and other traditions also grew around food as when freshmen invited seniors to dinner or the students invited the faculty. Some food activity was very informal – midnight feasts and chaffing dish parties (after hours cooking and sharing of food).

28

Some became quite sophisticated as when in 1914 the juniors and freshmen invited the seniors and sophomores to a Japanese dinner party, or in 1913 when Alpha Sigma entertained Kappa Chi at a "children's party." An emphasis on good appetite was part of the women's college scene before the 1920s and D'Youville students certainly were enthusiastic participants.[35]

If the food culture introduced a bit of levity into student activities, this was reinforced by physical culture at the college. In 1913, a senior dance was initiated. The students also organized an athletic tournament of relay and obstacle races, and by 1913, the school had an athletic association and a new set of tennis courts. In 1913, riding classes were introduced (but there is no indication they succeeded). Alpha Sigma broke the high-tone culture to raise money with a vaudeville show.[36]

Classes were small in the first decade, starting with only six and having nineteen graduates in 1919. Yet these young women took courses, edited the *D'Youville Magazine*, engaged in many school activities, and simply had fun with each other. Their energy translated into action in the future. By 1919, several had gone on to graduate school – Alice Mulhern who finished an MA at Cornell University, and Geraldine Helfter who was working on one there. In 1914, graduates swept the first three places in the English examination for Buffalo teachers and placed first and third in mathematics. In 1919, ten alumnae were teaching in high schools (two only as substitutes). One alumna taught piano at Lake Forest University School of Music. Mary Chabot worked for Catholic relief agencies in Europe during World War I and stayed to work in reconstruction in France. She later taught at a U.S. soldiers' high school in Germany where she was joined by another alumna. Several also entered business, one with the Federal Reserve Bank in Buffalo. Alumnae did marry – one even married an instructor after she had graduated. By 1919, it was clear that Bishop Colton's prodding and Grey Nun action had established a viable college.[37]

29

[1] Reverend Edward Dunn, "A Gymnasium in Buffalo: The Early Years of Canisius College," *Urban Education* Vol 8 (June 1984) 420-437.

[2] Sister R. P. Smith, p. 17. Sister Mary Sheila Driscol, "Those Early Years, Sowers of the Seed."

[3] Grande and Eberle, p. 87-93, 129.

[4] C. Golden and L. Katz. "The Shaping of Higher Education, 1890-1940." *Journal of Economic Perspectives* 13 (Winter 1999). Leonard Sweet. "The Female Seminary Movement and Women's Mission in Antebellum America." *Church History* 54 (March 1985) 4-55. Andrea Hamilton. *A Vision for Girls, Gender, Education and the Bryn Mawr School.* Baltimore: Johns Hopkins University Press, 2004, p. 11-12. John R. Thelin. *A History of American Higher Education.* Baltimore: Johns Hopkins University Press, 2004, p. 55-60. Paulson, Susan, and Loretta Higgins. "Gender, Co-Education and the Transformation in American Catholic Higher Education." *Catholic Historical Review*, 89 (July 2003). Grande and Eberle, p. 134-135.

[5] Sister R. P. Smith, p. 17-18; Sister Mary Kathleen Duggan, p. 17.

[6] *D'Youville Magazine*, 2:3.

[7] Toby Appel. "Physiology in American Women's Colleges: The Rise and Decline of a Female Sub-Culture." *Isis* 85 (March 1994) 26-56; and Sarah Gordon. "Smith College Students: The First Ten Classes, 1879-1888." *History of Education Quarterly*, Summer, 149-167.

[8] Kathleen Mahoney. *Catholic Higher Education in Protestant America, Jesuits and Harvard in the Age of the University.* Baltimore: Johns Hopkins University Press, 2003. passim.

[9] *D'Youville Magazine*, 6:1 (1915) p. 52 and 6:2 (1916) p. 130-1.

[10] *D'Youville Magazine*, 8:1 (1917) p. 75.

[11] *D'Youville Magazine*, 7:3 (1917) p. 180 and 8:1 (1918) p. 66-70.

[12] *D'Youville Magazine*, 9:2 (1918) advertisement. D. F. Frank, E. Schofer, and F. C. Torres, "Rethinking History: Change in University

Curriculum, 1910-1990," *Sociology of Education*, 67 (October 1994) p. 231-42.

[13] *D'Youville Magazine*, 8:2 (1919) p. 141. Joellen Watson. "Higher Education for Women in the United States: A Historical Perspective." *Educational Studies*, 8 (Summer 1977) p. 142. Susan B. Carter. "Academic Women Revisited, 1890-1963." *Journal of Social History*, 14 (Summer 1981).

[14] Sally Schwage. "Educating Women in American." *Signs*, 12 (Winter 1987) 333-72. Sweet (1985) p. 44-55. Lynn Gordon. "Annie Nathan Meyers and Barnard College." *History of Education Quarterly*, 26 (Winter, 1986) 503-522. *D'Youville Magazine*, 1:1 (1908) p. 35-38.

[15] Swager (1987); Gordon (1986); Christine Murray. "Teaching as a Profession: The Rochester Case in Historical Perspective." *Harvard Educational Review*, 62 (Winter 1992), 499-501.

[16] *Dimensions* (Spring 2006) p. 20-23 – reprinted from *D'Youville Magazine*, 4 (1912).

[17] *D'Youville Magazine*, 1:1 (1908) and 8:1 (1918).

[18] *D'Youville Magazine*, 3:3 (1911). Gordon, p. 149-167. *Historical Statistical History of the United States*. Stanford: Fairfield Publishers, 1965, p. 91. *D'Youville Magazine*, 3 (Number 4), 1911.

[19] *D'Youville Magazine*, 1:4, 2:1, 3:2, 5:1, 9:4.

[20] *D'Youville Magazine*, 2:1, 2:1, 5:1, 9:3, 8:1, 8:1.

[21] *D'Youville Magazine*, 1:2, 6:2, 7:4, 2:2, 5:1, 5:1, 6:2, 5:1, 7:2, 9:3, 6:2, 3:1, 5:3.

[22] *D'Youville Magazine*, 4:3; 5:1 p. 55-6; 6:4; 3:4. Linda Risenzweig. "The Anchor of My Life: Middle Class American Mothers and College Educated Daughters." *Journal of Social History*, 25 (Fall 1991).

[23] *D'Youville Magazine*, 1:2, 2:1, 2:2, 2:2, and 3:4.

[24] *D'Youville Magazine*, 1:2, 6:2, 6:3, 3:4, and 7:4.

[25] *D'Youville Magazine*, passim and 2:3; 3:3 p. 26-7; 3:4; and 6:4.

[26] *D'Youville Magazine*, 4:4 p. 14-19; 6:1 p. 27-31; 6:2 p. 61-71; 9:1; 9:4; 10:3; 2:1 p. 41; 3:2; 8:3; 9:4.

[27] *D'Youville Magazine*, 7:1 p. 3-7, 31-35; 7:3; 7:4 p. 194-99; 8:2; 8:3; 10:1.

[28] *D'Youville Magazine*, vol. 1-10 passim.

[29] *D'Youville Magazine*, 3:2, 8:2, 7:4, 8:1 and 3:3.

[30] *D'Youville Magazine*, 4:1 (1911) p. 39, 41; 2:1 (1909) p. 48-49; 3:1 (1910) p. 56-7; 3:2 (1910) p. 54-56; 6:4 (1914) p. 261-2; 6:2 (1914) p. 129; 7:1 (1914) p. 65-6.

[31] *D'Youville Magazine*, 2:2 (1910) p. 64-5; 2:1 (1909) p. 27. See Appel 1994; *D'Youville Magazine*, 3:4 (1911) p. 61-65; 2:3 (1910) p. 57. *D'Youville Magazine*, 2:2 (1910) p. 64-5; 2:1 (1909) p. 27. See Appel 1994; *D'Youville Magazine*, 3:4 (1911) p. 61-65; 2:3 (1910) p. 57.

[32] *D'Youville Magazine*, 4:1 (1911) p. 37-8; 4:4 (1912) p. 44-47; 4:4 (1912) p. 42-3; 6:3 (1914) p. 197; 7:4 (1915) p. 45; 8:2 (1917) p. 141.

[33] *D'Youville Magazine*, 3:3 (1911) p. 51-2; 5:3 (1913) p. 52-3; 7:1 (1914) p. 65-6; 7:3 (1915) p. 182-4; 8:3 (1917) p. 181.

[34] *D'Youville Magazine*, 3:1 (1910) p. 58-60; 8:1 (1916) p. 73-5; 4:2 (1912) p. 33; 7:2 (1915) p. 34.

[35] *D'Youville Magazine*, 4:2 (1912) p. 33; 5:3 (1913) p. 52-3; 6:2 (1914) p. 129; 3:2 (1911) p. 58; 3:3 (1911) p. 51-2. Margaret Lowe, *Looking Good: College Women and Body Image, 1875-1930* (Baltimore: Johns Hopkins 2003) passim. *D'Youville Magazine*, 4:2 (1912) p. 33; 5:3 (1913) p. 52-3; 6:2 (1914) p. 129; 3:2 (1911) p. 58; 3:3 (1911) p. 51-2. Margaret Lowe, *Looking Good: College Women and Body Image, 1875-1930* (Baltimore: Johns Hopkins 2003) passim.

[36] *D'Youville Magazine*, 5:3 (1913) p. 52-3; 6:1 (1913) p. 52-4; 7:3 (1915) p. 182-4; 9:2 (1918) p. 118-19.

[37] *D'Youville Magazine*, 6:4 (1914) p. 261-262; 9:4 (1920) p. 228-30.

Chapter Two

An Age of Excess and D'Youville's Response

The 1920s (the Roaring '20s, the Jazz Age, the return to normalcy) was a time of ambiguity. The images of F. Scott Fitzgerald in both *This Side of Paradise* and *The Great Gatsby* continue to define the standards of the age. Young men returning from World War I wished to extend the spirit of adventure and had a taste for a more glamorous, less provincial world. Young women responded with a more blatant sexuality expressed mainly in fashion and style. Everyone was in love with the automobile – its speed, its extension of personal control. Everyone listened to jazz and danced to a new, stronger rhythm with oft changing steps. Everyone was young – this 1920s was the age of youth. But the 1920s was also a "return to normalcy," the slogan used by Republicans to dominate the political scene. The businessman was the heroic ideal in this new world that preached materialism. Fundamentalist Protestants disagreed with the heady and materialist emphasis and founded the beginning of a deeply conservative religious attitude. They rejected science and made it illegal to teach evolution in Tennessee, resulting in the noted Scopes trial. A new Ku Klux Klan grew with a racist, anti-Semitic, and anti-Catholic doctrine of hate – they were strong enough to dominate politics, not just in the South but in Indiana (with other incursions into the North). Such nativist sentiment helped create immigration restriction modeled and aimed mostly at immigrants from Catholic countries. How does a small Catholic women's college fare in such a turbulent era?

By 1921 D'Youville published a yearbook with individual pictures that were gathered into a formal picture of the class. Note the neck stocks as well as the cap and gown of the seniors. ————

This is a less formal picture of the members of the class of 1921.

The aspect of the 1920s that affected D'Youville most was the tremendous growth of college and secondary school enrollments. Enrollment in college went up two and a half times; enrollment in secondary schools by a multiple of six. Since many D'Youville graduates became secondary school teachers this growth was reflected at D'Youville.[1] Enrollment at D'Youville grew from 104 (pictured in yearbook) in 1921 to 204 in 1929. The number graduating grew from twenty-one to fifty-four similar to the national average growth of 250%.[2] In the boom of the 1920s, women's enrollment generally remained high and women were 47.3% of college students. College students set the tone of a youth culture which filtered down to high school students as well. This was a short distance at D'Youville since Holy Angels Academy and the college shared the same building until 1929, when growth of both dictated that a new facility be built for Holy Angels Academy in the solidly middle-class neighborhood at the northern edge of the city.

The youth culture of the 1920s revolved around college life and style. At the center were young men and women organized in fraternities and sororities. These organizations, each with separate living quarters, marshaled their members to dominate the social and athletic lives of the college, which in their eyes was the real purpose of college. Extracurricular activities, the students felt, trained them to operate in the world of business while academic subjects were simply a waste of time – one needed to pass and not much more. Ideas about competition or learning to work with ones peers were what fraternities and sororities taught. Prestige came through multiple campus activities (or through leadership in a critical activity – football hero, prom queen, etc.). Leaders always understood the new implications of peer culture – the dress, the current dance step, the right automobile. Peer culture, of course, created homogeneity, but one that was at odds with parental views and sometimes with views of college officials. Living away from home, particularly in the independence of a fraternity or sorority house, let college students establish their own modes of dress and social behavior, including sexual behavior. Such behaviors were not radically different from those in the more general society, but they were somewhat less restrictive.[3]

Social life at D'Youville both reflected and rejected this new college culture while sharing the growth that made it possible. Sororities were founded in its first decade, but they did not have an independent

33

existence or practice exclusivity. Meetings and "spreads" were done in the Club Room of the college. All the young women were inducted into Alpha Sigma by the junior class in a week of moderate hazing – having to carry books or dress in children's clothing. The sophomores were with the seniors in Kappa Chi, a second sorority. The sororities were used to define class status and to unite the college across yearly classes. Alumni organized "passive" chapters of the two sororities and reported on luncheons, bridge parties, dances, and formal dinners. Sorority activity included providing "spreads" for their members to enjoy, but also active charitable work. Throughout the decade the young women of Alpha Sigma provided a Christmas party and gifts for the children at the Father Baker houses, and sometimes at the Saint Joseph's Orphanage. Kappa Chi aided the Mount Carmel Guild to provide Christmas festivities in that parish in the early 1920s; later they worked with the Women's Auxiliary of the Saint Vincent DePaul Society and provided Christmas parties for the Saint Mary's Home. The passive chapters used funds from their social activities to aid similar charities.[4] Sorority life at D'Youville was alive but also differed from the national foci of sororities – it was less independent, less exclusive, and more oriented to service.

Classes grew through the 1920s but the style of picture did not alter. ——————————

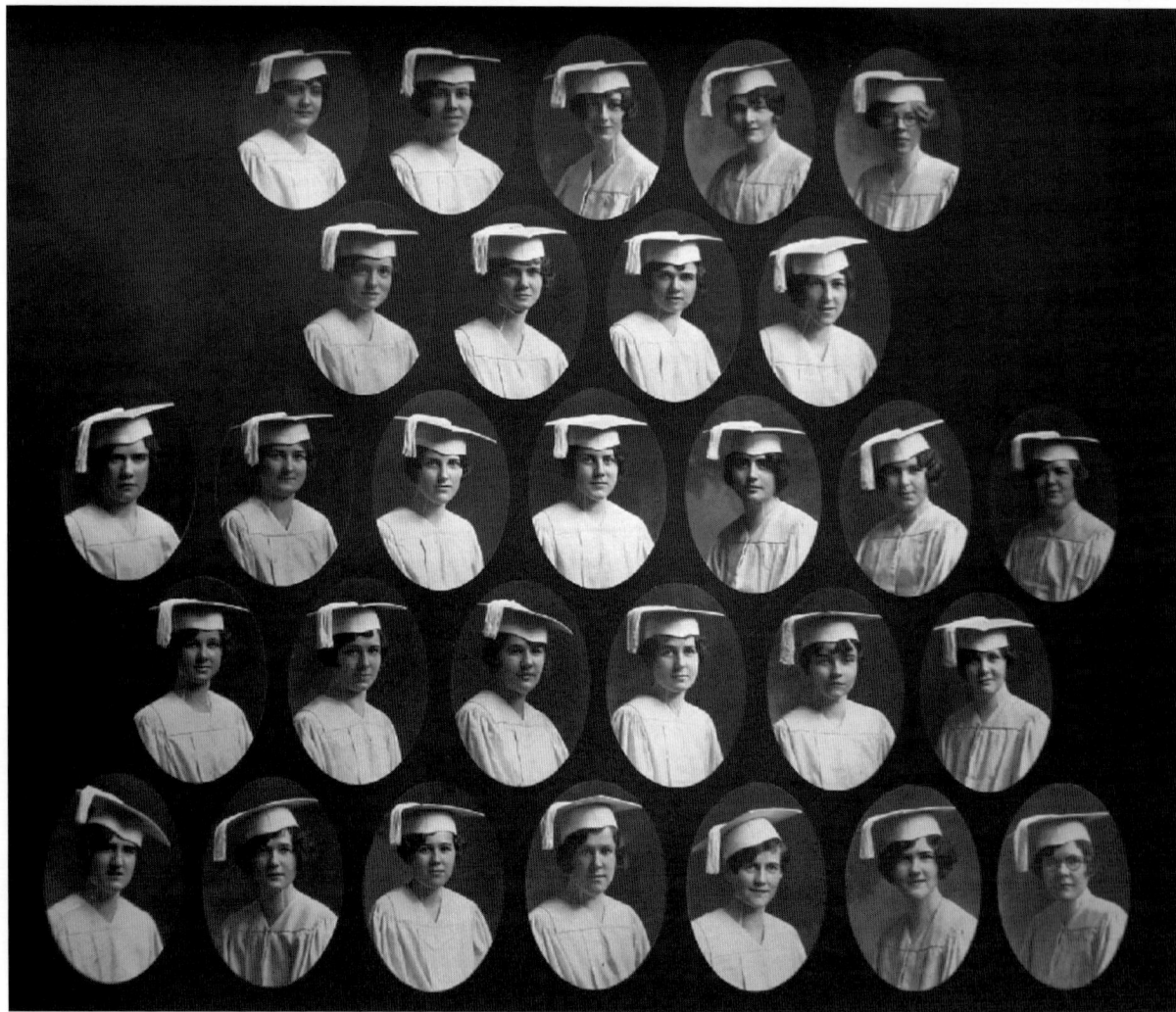

34

The college library in the 1920s included style, comfort, art objects, and few religious connotations—also relatively few books.

Students of the 1920s were active in student affairs other than sororities and fraternities. D'Youville women followed this trend. The *D'Youvillian* (the yearbook) lists a minimum of seven and a maximum of fourteen organizations over the decade. Some of this fluctuation reflected real reduction in student activity but much of it was simply non-inclusion in the yearbook. For example, the Newman Literary Society published the *D'Youville Magazine* throughout the decade but was only mentioned in 1921. Some groups, like the editorial board of the *D'Youvillian*, the Student Government, the Student Honor Council, and the sororities were always listed; others might be dropped for a year or a note might indicate that the organization was inactive. At most schools in the 1920s sports and pep clubs dominated student life – little of that existed at D'Youville. The young women organized basketball teams by year level and by the late 1920s a game between the juniors and seniors was a large event, held at the Armory. (D'Youville had no gym and tennis courts were its sole athletic facility.) They donated funds from the event to the Student Foreign Missions Crusade. The one club D'Youville shared with other colleges was a dramatic society which each year put on a spring play. Drama was social and intellectual. Many of the other clubs at D'Youville recognized intellectual interests – with

The religious aspect of the college came out in the richly appointed chapel (as it was in 1922). Notice the communion rail across the width of the altar. ————————

a French club, Le Cercle Francais, and a Spanish club, El Club Castellan. (The French club always put on a play in the original language and the Spanish club often did so as well.)

A Contemporary History Club held debates – in 1928 they debated whether the United States was imperialist to a positive conclusion. Students organized a Classic Club in 1922 which actively examined less well known texts through the remainder of the decade. Science students had an association where students presented papers. The rich musical heritage of the college was obvious in the 1929 yearbook when the Glee Club with forty-five singers and four accompanists was pictured. An instrumental ensemble of five girls sometimes joined them, and also entertained at a Convention of National Catholic

Alumnae which came to Buffalo, played twice on radio broadcasts, and played for charity banquets and at the state hospital.[5]

D'Youville women also put emphasis on religion and service. The Children of Mary was such a part of tradition that it was only mentioned in 1921 and 1929. The students of Foreign Mission Crusade came to Buffalo Catholic Colleges in 1924 and D'Youville had its own chapter by 1927. D'Youville women joined Girl Scout training classes revived at the college in 1925, and by 1927 ten women were helping to lead Girl Scout troops. In 1928, they began social work with the Ladies Auxiliary of the Saint Vincent DePaul Society.[6]

D'Youville women might not have engaged in quite the same activities as students at secular colleges or big state universities but they were very active. Senior listing of activities showed a range of activities over their four years at the college from four to twenty-five activities. (In 1927, there was one senior who listed no activities.) The median number of activities ranged from six to nine in 1927 – or most students were in one or two clubs every year (only offices in the sororities were counted since everyone belonged). Some could be incredibly active. A total of twenty-five meant that a young woman averaged more than six clubs every year of her college life.[7]

Like other students of the 1920s, the D'Youville women were activists (if with a slightly different orientation) – in attitude they sometimes fully reflected their peers. The D'Youville seniors organized the first prom for the juniors in 1920. In 1921 the prom was held at the Lafayette Hotel "with an unexpectedly large attendance." It started at 9 p.m., broke for a midnight dinner,

> Like other students of the 1920s, the D'Youville women were ACTIVISTS (if with a slightly different orientation) – in attitude they sometimes FULLY REFLECTED their peers.

and then dancing continued until 3 a.m. By 1927, the venue for the prom became the largest hotel in Buffalo and attendance had risen to 250 couples. The students involved the alumnae as patronesses and the alumnae obviously attended since total school attendance was not that large.[8] The young women loved to dance. Senior comments reflected that "dancing fascinated her as you will note if you sometimes look into the club rooms." "Proms are her forte. However, before going to them she insists upon giving a dissertation on the undesirability of high heels." "When there is music . . . we can positively state that no step has yet been invented that Kathryn could not master." And the music was jazz – "She can play the piano, both jazz music and classical like no one else." In 1927 the senior essay waxed eloquently on the prom:

> The relative merits of pink taffeta with rose velvet bows, robe de style, and of a silhouette model effectively carried out in black velvet with a dash of rhinestones, are duly considered. Black is so intriguing – that note of sophistication lends enchantment to blond or brunette – but still, HE advises pale pink, so pale pink it is . . . 'Wasn't it wonderful?' 'The dress was beautiful, but _____' 'I never knew she was so pretty before.' 'Did you see him, ___ blue eyes, crisp curly hair, a blond?' 'Stunning.' 'Marvelous.' 'Delicious.'[9]

THE PIETA in the college chapel. The chapel was used often by students and was the place of the annual retreat that each class undertook.

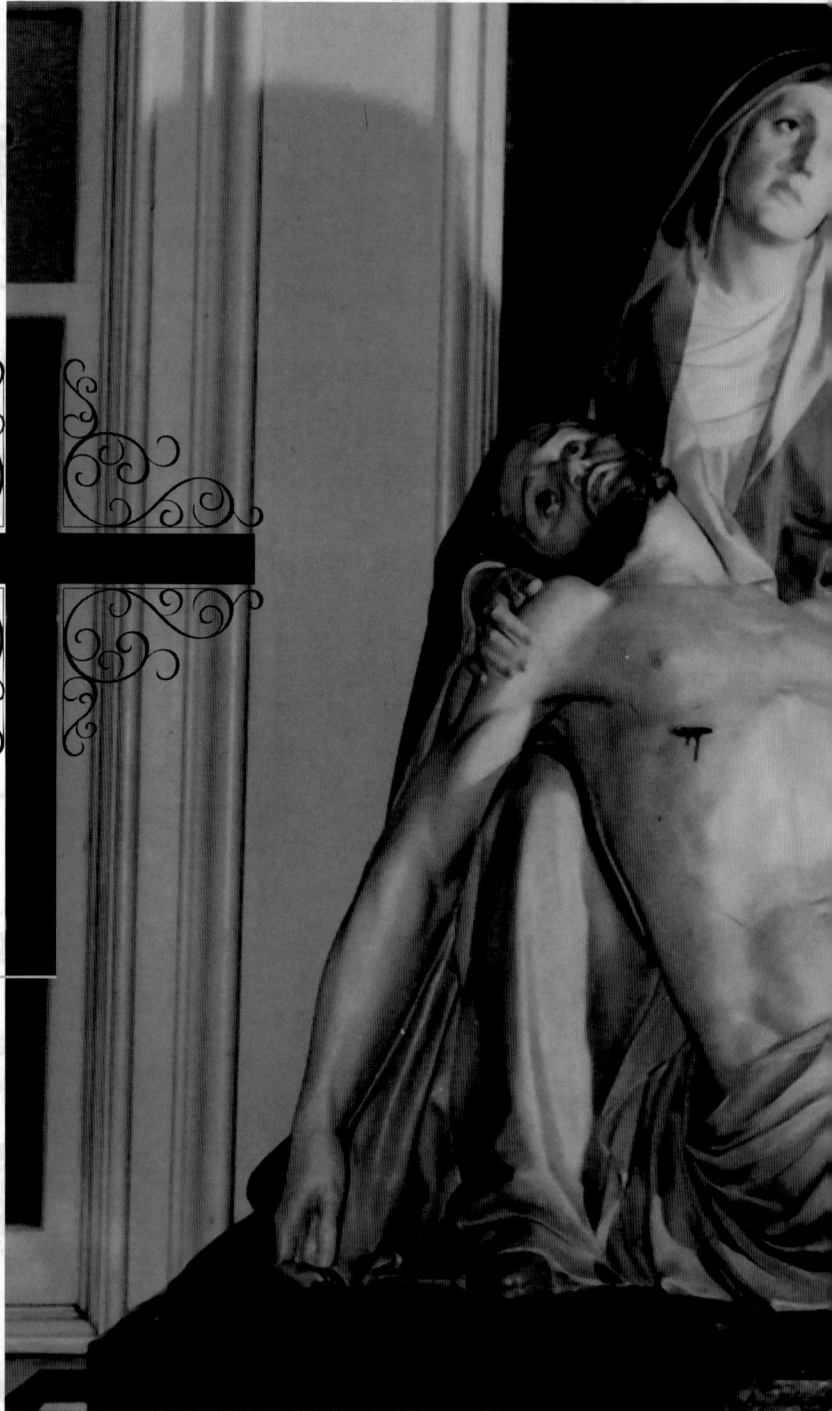

40

Students in small groups for 1929. They dressed quite in fashion, fur abounds and hair is much shorter; one can see lower legs, but these were very modest clothes for the 1920s.

As the quote denotes, D'Youville women tried to be fashionable – in 1927 eight of the eleven seniors pictured wore fur coats or fur collars. An alumna from the 1920s, when questioned about the fur coats, said that her sisters insisted she be like everyone else and bought the coat for her, even though they had little money themselves. Although earlier pictures showed elaborate if sometimes short hair styles, by the late 1920s, all the young women wore some form of the "bob." In 1926, the senior essay quotes a math major classmate:

> 'I saw the best-looking dress today,' says Helen, as she proceeds to give a detailed account of the newest creation that so-and-so are showing, enumerating style, color, and so on for all interested parties; has she ever yet missed a fashion show? [In 1929, another senior was complimented.] There is the trimness of her slimness, the swagger of her clothes, the candor and fairness of herself. [10]

Although young men seemed to be admired in relation to the prom, they drew some critical comment. The yearbook noted of one senior in 1921, "She simply can't be bored except by pork and Irishmen." Another in 1922 was called a future dean and "even for the sake of Junior prom and Senior dance, she cannot tolerate men." A joke printed in 1924 told of a professor reading "by no means was he polished or refined" and a student, sotto voce, saying "another uncut gem." In the end, males seem to win as a senior prediction in 1928 noted, "Well, Mr. Cupid seems to have taken that affair out of our hands."[11]

Automobiles were the energy of the 1920s; they produced a feeling of freedom. In 1923, the class president could "get enough automobiles to take the whole college for a ride." In 1927, the yearbook printed a short poem:

> O! To have a little Ford
> To own the rumble seat and all.
> A well filled tank and four good tires,
> That I might answer the robin's call.

Cars became extensions of personality. A senior was seen "driving up the avenue in her beloved Hup." Or "Mary's Ford is more than just a car, it is an institution, for those folks who are late for a downtown appointment, or for school in the morning."[12]

They danced, played jazz, dressed well, were feeling their way toward gender relationships, loved their cars, and they had fun. "She does calculus for recreation, but she doesn't object to puns or parties." "She will never refuse an opportunity to go skating and is always ready to plan class parties." They followed the fads of crossword puzzles and played bridge. In all, "we have reached the ultimate conclusion that D'Youville girls are the happiest, most studious and lighthearted girls whom we have ever met."[13]

Some social aspects separated D'Youville from the ordinary college scene of the 1920s. Since all girls belonged to the sororities there was no snobbism about belonging. The split that developed between commuters and residents at large campuses was addressed consciously – as when after a class party at the home of a commuter all boarders went home with a commuter for a visit. The revolution in sexuality that occurred in the 1920s (toward experimentation between those who thought of themselves as engaged) may or may not have influenced D'Youville women.[14]

In activities and styles, the D'Youville women showed modest differences within trends of the 1920s. Some contrasts were sharper. While college women at large institutions retreated from difficult subjects and half moved into the gender pure space of home economics, D'Youville retained a rigorous curriculum with respect granted to those who majored in subjects like mathematics. Relatively few students continued to produce the *D'Youville Magazine* throughout the decade. The graduates retained a strong commitment to teaching. In 1921, forty-two alumnae were teaching in high schools – in all fields including mathematics and science but most strongly in English, languages, and Latin. In 1925, eleven of twenty-five graduates joined just two public high schools. Home economics wasn't even taught at D'Youville.[15]

Religion was attacked on many college campuses with struggle over compulsory chapel at Trinity College (becoming Duke University). Revivals were mocked; only a periphery of students clung to tradition. This was not the picture at D'Youville. The first yearbook in 1921 was dedicated to "the Grey Nuns who fostered us." Six of the next nine were dedicated to individual sisters and one to the chancellor, Bishop William Turner of Buffalo. Only in 1926 (with an abbreviated yearbook with no dedication) and 1928 (dedicated to "Our Parents") were there exceptions. The 1923 yearbook, with the second dedication to Reverend Mother Mary Augustine (a former president) read:

> In Loving Memory of Mother Mary Augustine. She was of the great race of those who startle our common days by their great-hearted and high-souled lives. Her name to all who knew her must always be associated with everything that is wise, kindly, pure, tender, and good. To the duties of her consecrated state of life she gave the unflagging service of a heart of love with the love of God.[16]

Each class had a three-day religious retreat every year. The retreat master changed through the decade, but was always noted among the faculty. The class histories always mentioned these retreats with great fondness. The following schedule was typical for a day of a retreat:

42

Sport was limited at D'Youville in the 1920s, but this group of young women celebrate a basketball victory in 1929.

8:45 Mass and Sermon

10:00 Stations of the Cross

10:30 Retreat Master Talked

Private Devotions

11:50 Spiritual reading by class

Visit to Blessed Sacrament

2:00 Conferences

3:30 Sermon, benediction

The retreat was described in the following manner:

> Not that there was less of gaiety and merriment, but it was of a different nature – that
> interior joy which manifests itself on the very countenances of those whose hearts are filled
> to overflowing with the love of God.[17]

Perhaps some of this religious feeling came with the origins of the students. At the beginning of the 1920s (1923), a third of the graduates were alumnae of the Holy Angels Academy and sixty had graduated from there or other Catholic high schools, mainly in the Buffalo area. Of the graduates in 1929, only 17% had attended Holy Angels but 52% were still from Catholic high schools in Buffalo and another 15% came from non-Buffalo Catholic high schools. Catholic academies in Ogdensbury and Philadelphia also run by the Grey Nuns contributed more strongly to the student body by the end of the 1920s. Students from public high schools were mainly Catholic but hadn't experienced the intensity of religious feeling and instruction available in the Catholic system.[18]

The faculty of the college also reflected this Catholic atmosphere. In 1921, of the faculty pictured or listed in the yearbook, twelve of twenty were religious – eleven sisters and a priest. The priest taught philosophy, the sisters taught music and languages. Later they would teach mathematics and some classics. Dr. Lappin dominated English; Mr. Dawson, Classics; and Mr. Curtin, Science. Physical Education always had a female instructor. By the end of the 1920s, only sixteen faculty were listed but eight were still sisters and one a priest. The students had good reasons for thanking the Grey Nuns for their education and dedicating yearbooks to them.[19]

One aspect of the college life and activity did change under the influence of Dr. Lappin. The content of the *D'Youville Magazine* took on a quite different orientation. Short stories almost disappeared as did Catholic cultural material. Early in the twenties the most common article was on English literature but with a great deal more interest in critics (rather obscure Catholic women writers still drew comment). Conrad was the single most popular writer in this decade. What replaced the short story was an interest in more realistic prose – writing of travels or simple vignettes of what was occurring around town, in the five and dime store, or at the "Bobber" shop or on Lafayette Square. These were rare pieces in the teens. Music had its articles. The solar eclipse of 1925 drew four serious articles on astronomy. History and politics got some attention. Ethnic political attitudes were displayed: Wilson's death was noted with compassion and Mussolini's rise to power was lauded. The journal showed young women interested in a variety of subjects – although English majors clearly predominated.[20]

43

D'Youville students of the 1920s loved to dance, did all the fads, and appreciated style and clothes. They were as interested in campus activity as anyone at college, but these activities often had a religious and service aspect. Religion was neither mocked nor ignored and in this they were in the minority among college students. They seemed to take teachers and curriculum seriously (but this was usually more the case for women than for men). Their object in school remained focused on the teaching profession. They were of their generation but also slightly separate from it. What effect would the Great Depression have?

[1] Paula Fauss, *The Damned and the Beautiful: America Youth in the 1920s*. NY: Oxford, 1972, p. 119-167.

[2] *D'Youvillian*, 1921, 1929. Meeting of the Board of Governors 1912-1964. D'Youville College Archive.

[3] Fauss. Passim.

[4] *D'Youvillian*, 1924, p. 96; also 1922, 1923, 1925, 1929.

[5] *D'Youvillian*, 1921-1929.

[6] *D'Youvillian*, 1921, 1924, 1925, 1927, 1928, 1929.

[7] *D'Youvillian*, 1923, 1925-1929.

[8] *D'Youville Magazine*, 12:1 (1992), p. 3; 17:1 (1927), p. 42.

[9] *D'Youvillian*, 1927, p. 25; 1923, p. 27; 1927, p. 38; 1929, p. 39; and 1927, p. 71.

[10] *D'Youvillian*, 1926, p. 14; 1929, p. 35. D'Youville Oral History Archive, Sister Florence Knab interview.

[11] *D'Youvillian*, 1921, p. 32; 1922, p. 28; 1924, p. 87; 1928, p. 46.

[12] *D'Youvillian*, 1923, p. 24; 1927, p. 139; 1927, p. 36; 1928, p. 23.

[13] *D'Youvillian*, 1921, p. 33; 1922, p. 39; 1925, p. 29; 1927, p. 38-9; 1924, p. 96.

[14] Fauss, p. 119-167, p. 260-290. *D'Youvillian*, 1923, p. 46.

[15] Margaret Lowe. *Looking Good: College Women & Body Image, 1875-1930*, p. 111. *D'Youville Magazine*, vol. 11:4, p. 212, 214; vol. 15:3, p. 142.

[16] *D'Youvillian*, 1923; also 1921, 1922, 1924, 1925, 1926, 1927, 1928, 1929. Fauss, p. 119-167.

[17] *D'Youville Magazine*, 15:4 (1925), p. 40-41. *D'Youvillian* – the decade.

[18] *D'Youvillian*, 1923, 1924, 1925, 1927, 1928, 1929.

[19] *D'Youvillian*, 1921-1928.

[20] *D'Youville Magazine*, 11-18 (1921-1929). See especially 17:4, 18:2, 18:4, 14:3, 16:4.

Chapter Three

Impacts of the 1930s

This is the class of 1932. The picture represents the nostalgia for the 1920s. A note in the college magazine states that they rounded up every fur coat in the college to take this picture. ——————————

How depressing was the Depression on the life of D'Youville College? Our vision of the 1930s is that the stock market crashed in 1929 and the country tumbled after. Actually, it was a long slow decline to a depth in 1933, then some recovery to 1936, another drop in 1938, and finally, war production ending the economic problems. But many folks had jobs during the Depression. Employment, though it may have been partial, statistically held up while unemployment rose. Colleges continued to enroll students; indeed, D'Youville's enrollment grew from 215 in 1929 to 300 in 1939, or 40%. Women's colleges generally did well, with the high point of female enrollment in those years.[1]

The young women at D'Youville seemed to desire to forget the Depression. Many aspects of student life and attitudes reflected this. "Rise late enough to limit breakfast to half a cup of coffee, thus making one able to sympathize with sufferers from economic depression."[2] The quote at least acknowledges the Depression but attitudes toward cars, consumption, and dress reflected the 1920s. "Gone is the great, gray Franklin. No more will happy, young laughter echo forth from the region of the tool chest." Young women tried to stay slim. The introduction to a sorority dessert sale read: "We intend to make everyone forget to count the calories when they see the tempting display." "All the raccoon coats in the school managed to get into that picture, which promises to be a rare and wondrous thing." And in terms of attitude (after a strong religious introduction), "In spring a freshman's fancy lightly turns to thoughts – new clothes, tennis, horseback riding, vacations, exams, love." "The early morning classes, the girlish confidences, the argumentative lunch, the convenience of green lacquered society rooms, the post mortem of the night before."[3]

Through the first three years of the Depression, the prom remained a yearly focus, held at the luxurious Statler. "The prom. Just what 'he said' and 'she said' and how stunning, divinely different . . . we all

> " The prom. Just what 'HE SAID' and 'SHE SAID' and how stunning, DIVINELY DIFFERENT...we all looked. "

looked." Even though the prom was abandoned in the later 1930s, tea dances (with young men from Canisius) were established. By the late 1930s, the young women were into new fads like swing and the jitterbug. The school also introduced a series of lectures on personal presentation and etiquette in the later 1930s to ensure D'Youville graduates could join society.[4]

As all this denotes, D'Youville women looked for a good time. One alumna remembered a great college prank. She and some friends painted the toenails of a life-size plaster cast of the Maid of Orleans – the recently sainted Jeanne d'Arc – bright red. (The cast remains outside the college theater with no trace of the prank.) The class was disciplined with the curtailment of privileges, but no one named the perpetrators. The same alumna was named in the college magazine as organizing a grand trip to Cleveland for the Navy-Notre Dame football game, while many other girls attended local football games. Football may have been declining at schools like Harvard and the University of Chicago, but it kept the appeal of the 1920s in Buffalo. D'Youville women also continued to play basketball and tennis among themselves (the school did have an outdoor basketball court by the 1930s as well as tennis courts and continued to hire the Armory on a regular basis).[5]

Like the 1920s, D'Youville women maintained a tremendous interest in school activities. Looking at reported activity in the 1931 and 1938 yearbooks, and the intervening D'Youville issues of the magazine devoted to seniors, showed that the levels of activity remained as high as the 1920s. In 1931, the most active senior reported seven activities, the least active three activities, with a mean number of five activities. Actually, the number of activities reported seemed to rise in the 1930s, although some of the increase may have been how students listed their activities. In 1932, for example, there was a jump to the most active listing twenty-four activities, the least active five activities, and the mean number stood at nine activities. By the end of the 1930s, these numbers were forty-two for the most active, five for the least, with a mean of nineteen and one-half activities. Virtually all the clubs of the 1920s continued through the 1930s including the literary society which changed its name to the Alice Meynell, the French Club (now named for Jeanne D'Arc), the Spanish Club, Classic Club, history club, math club, science club, the two sororities (continuing their social service activities), the library club, the Glee Club, the Choir, and the Sodality of Mary. The students added a German club in the 1930s and a new honor society, Kappa Gamma Pi, for graduates of Catholic colleges, in 1930.[6]

47

Like the 1920s, much activity was oriented toward social service (the sororities still gave Christmas parties at Father Baker's) and to Catholicism. The Sodality of Mary was remembered as the most active organization by alumna. The Sodality had four separate committees: Eucharistic, Literature, Mission (which collected books for a small college in North Carolina), and Social Services (which later in the 1930s was preparing baskets of food for poor families) and had contact with the Catholic Worker group, reporting Dorothy Day's speech at a peace conference. In the early '30s, they cooperated with other colleges to provide five radio broadcasts. The Sodality even put on a program in 1937 to celebrate the 150th anniversary of the U.S. Constitution.[7]

At least in the early 1930s reports from the alumnae enforced the continuation of attitudes from the 1920s. Alumnae notes from 1930 showed sixteen women in teaching, five pursuing graduate studies, only five were in business, and two in social work. Three alumnae got married and two joined the sisterhood. In 1935, eighteen alumnae were teaching, eleven were in further school, and five were in business (by then entering teaching was getting more difficult). Alumnae also reported the usual style of activities: dances, dinners, teas, and card parties. An alumna also secured the Wanakah Country Club for the senior farewell dinner in 1934.[8]

While there was a strong student desire to keep the Depression at bay, the economic bad times did have effects. The *D'Youville Magazine* was slimmer; the *D'Youvillian* disappeared for six years. Interviews indicated that many struggled to pay the tuition which remained at $200 a year throughout the 1930s. "I think my father worked two and three jobs or whatever he could get because he had been working

In 1930 great elms covered the front lawn of the college. One student recalls watching the squirrels play in these trees during chemistry class.

in construction . . . then there was no construction. I don't think he paid his taxes at the time" (but he did keep his daughter in school). Another reported, "It was tough because my sister [was] a year ahead of me at D'Youville, my brother was two years in back of me at Canisius . . . My dad, of course was working but not making as much . . . My mother, she was stingy, too. She insisted that we had to have our education." The same alumna noted:

> We had to wear [an academic] gown in our senior year and I was glad because I couldn't compete with my other friends and dress as well as they did because during the depression mother couldn't do all of it, so we had hand-me-downs to wear. But in our senior year it didn't matter that much because everybody was dressed alike, and that was great. ·

Only one alumna indicated there were no problems with money because her "dad had his own barber shop and cigar store" (rather depression-proof occupations).[9]

All of these women had been commuter students perhaps to save money, but all remembered the commute fondly. Students from the northern suburbs (the Tonawanda's) rode the train together on the way to the University of Buffalo and Canisius as well as D'Youville. The same group gathered on Friday afternoon for drinks at the Park Lane (one of Buffalo's elegant restaurants) before going home. All remembered going to Hoefler's pastry shop on Connecticut for coffee, snacks, and perhaps an illicit cigarette. So while they didn't have much, they did have fun. The class predictions in 1936 indicated a desire to escape from the woes of the 1930s as classmates were named to be heads of businesses, airline pilots, NBC announcers, the head of Columbia University Sociology Department, and to marry into the aristocracy.[10]

One of D'Youville College's distinctions in the 1920s was a sense of religious purpose and interest. If anything, this religious sense deepened in the 1930s. Not only was the Sodality extremely active throughout the 1930s, but the retreats continued, students voluntarily came to school early to attend daily Mass, and one article in the magazine debated sleeping late or rising early to get to Mass, coming down on the side of virtue leading to good feeling for the day. (Interviews did note the daughter of a Lutheran minister was attending D'Youville in the 1930s.)[11]

> In 1933, Bishop Turner reminded the graduates of the value of their education:
>
> Today Protestants are striving here and there to recover the beautiful things that it destroyed long ago, but they are chasing the shadow, since they do not accept the substance. The substance is our Catholic Religion in all its completeness, in all its logic, in all its developed historic constancy. It is from that that one church derives its power to educate body, mind, and soul, sense and sentiment, taste and appreciation.

A few years later, a student editorial responded to a meeting of the presidents of major universities to discuss the place of theology in the university with this comment:

> We students of a Catholic College can sympathize with the problems of students in non-Catholic institutions – colleges and universities which avowedly teach truths, yet omit all mention of the supreme truths.[12]

49

Ivy, the vine of tradition, almost covered the front door in 1932.

By the 1930s the college was strong in the sciences. These cabinets display the physics equipment from 1939.

In May of 1931, the D'Youville girls tried to create a May Day celebration naming Mary as the queen of the May. That did not become a tradition, but in 1930, a Mass celebrated juniors moving up to become seniors, Moving Up Day (MUD), which did become tradition although it would lose most of its religious connotation.

The *D'Youville Magazine* called its December issue the Christmas Issue in the 1930s and it contained traditional Christmas lore or comments on how other cultures celebrated the holidays. Over the decade, Catholic cultural articles grew from three or four a year to eight or nine per year. It also carried editorials attacking popular culture for the loss of the spiritual value of Christmas and for violence and sordid content. In 1934, the magazine reported on student attendance at a conference of three thousand on Catholic School Action which called for the boycott of objectionable films. More significantly in 1934, students in Sodality helped organize a six-college symposium on the human side of saints and a few years later (1937) on the Historicity of the Gospels.[13]

Politics was very much a side issue in the 1920s, and even the decade before D'Youville students had shown only a slight interest. In the 1930s, the *D'Youville Magazine* reported more activities and in its articles (only modestly more common) suggested a heightened political awareness. These political questions were not recalled in alumni interviews. The politics reflected by D'Youville women was shaped by their Catholicism as well as by their position in society. One critical issue that affected college students was the civil war in Spain. While most college students supported republican Spain, the church took a sharply different view. The first hints of the difference appeared in an article on the Mexican revolution under Gardina. The expropriation movement was called communism. A letter in the *D'Youville Magazine* called for investigation of "persecuted Catholics in Mexico and . . . for the insults offered God in Russia." The same issue reported a Sodality symposium on communistic youth movement in Russia. The debate topic in 1935 was the viability of communism and in early 1936, all such ideas were rejected in a call to make the world safe for "Christology."[14] Spain

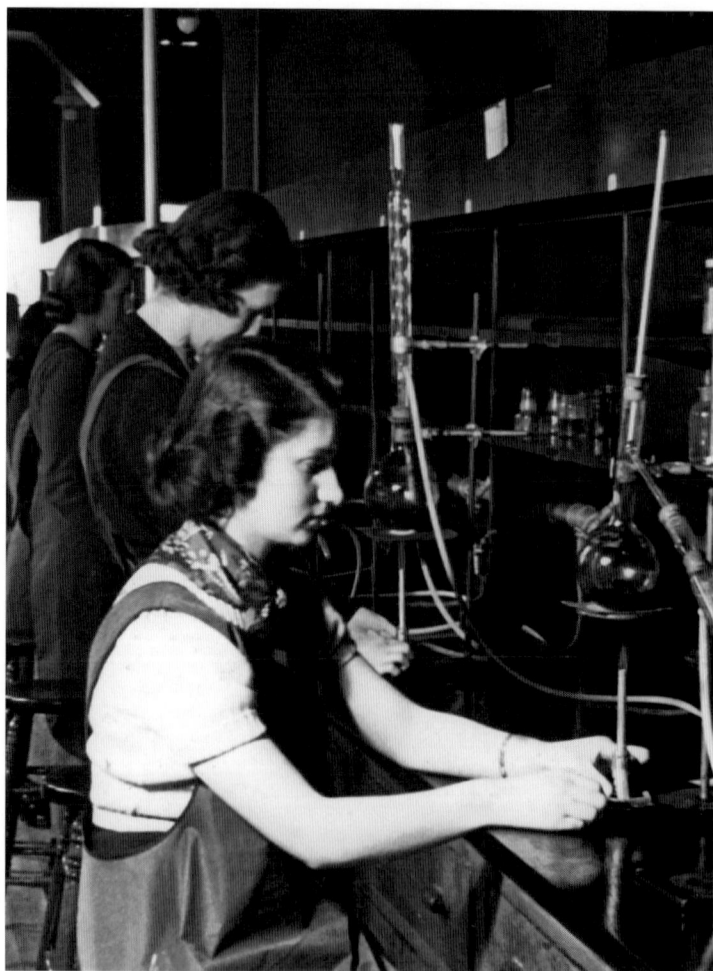

Students in 1939 hard at work in the chemistry lab. ⎯⎯⎯⎯⎯

52

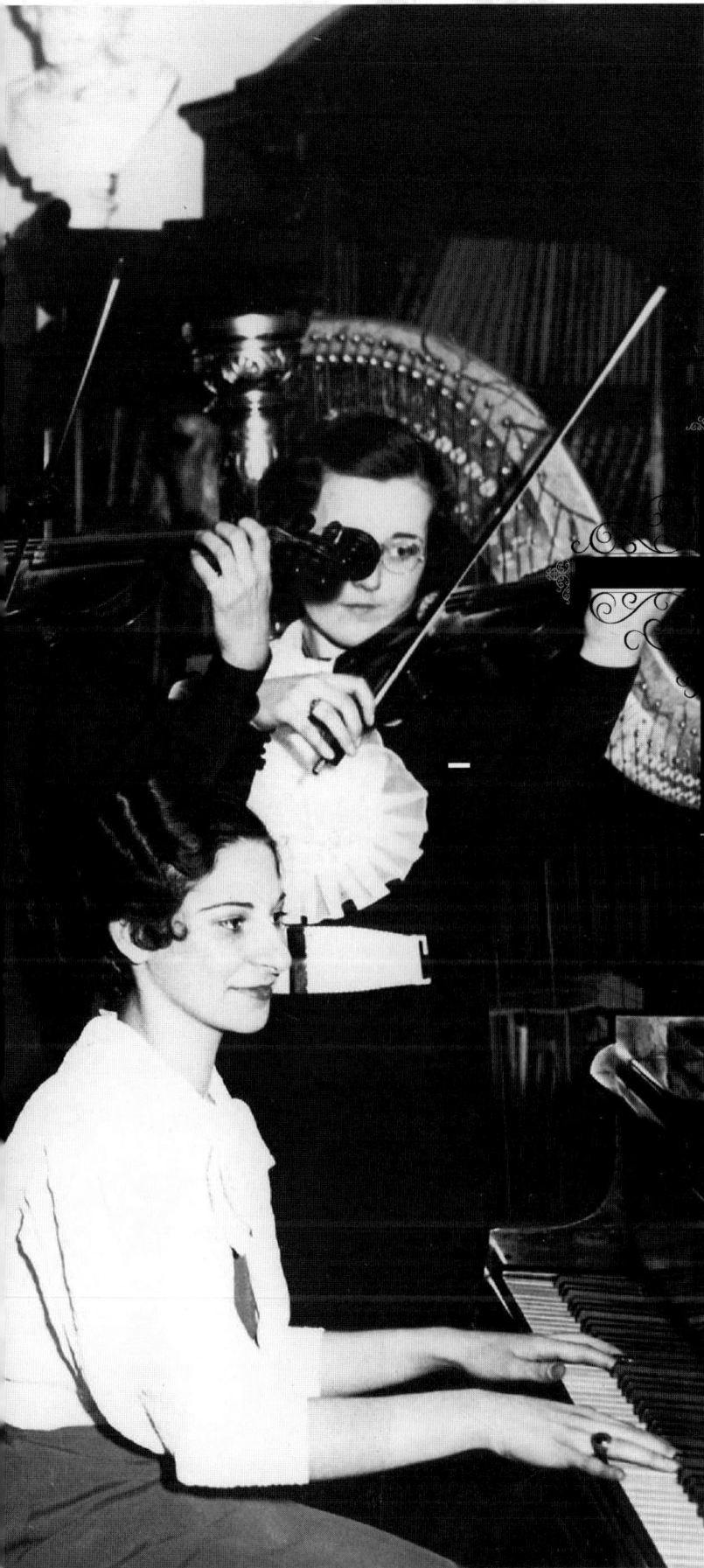

THE MUSIC ROOM, St Cecelia's Hall, could accommodate the practice of many instruments.

entered directly into these considerations in 1936 when an article claimed Benedictine monks were executed by the Republic. In 1937, Sister Saint Ignatius, D'Youville's only historian, lectured on Spain supporting Franco and condemning the Republic as communist. The debate did not end; two issues later the magazine ran parallel newspaper quotes condemning and supporting the Republic (the supporting quotes denied the Benedictine execution story). An editorial in the same issue disliked the German and Italian interventions. The question was settled in 1938 when the Catholic Church supported Franco and condemned his opponents as communists – a student article accepted this position.[15]

Spain was the critical area of difference; despite the comment on Mussolini in the 1920s, D'Youville students did not support fascism generally. In 1935, a student described sailing from Belgium to Spain on a ship under the Nazi flag with great feeling of discomfort. In 1936, Sodality sponsored a conference at D'Youville in interracial diversity. By 1938, the magazine denoted how Nazism ended the true celebration of Christmas and in the next issue an editorial condemned the German treatment of Jews and noted astutely that the same thing could happen to Catholics. As war gathered on the horizon in the fall of 1939, an editorial suggested the German people really didn't support the Nazis (remember D'Youville had an active German club and many of Buffalo's Catholics were of German origin).[16]

Like their opinion of Nazism, D'Youville students followed other American students in other areas of foreign affairs – generally supporting American neutrality. In 1935, the debate topic was on

The music program culminated in a rich choral tradition. This 1930 photo shows a high proportion of the college student body participating in Glee Club.

The editors of the college magazine posed for this formal picture in 1931.

The editors of the yearbook also posed in 1931. The Depression created a period when the yearbook became the final issue of the magazine and was quite abbreviated.

the neutrality laws and in 1936, an editorial in the magazine declared positive support. In 1937, D'Youville sent a delegation to a Model League of Nations held at Cornell (they represented Hungary). By 1939, they wrote supporting the peace advocacy of the pacifist Catholic Worker movement headed by Dorothy Day.[17]

Like the country as a whole, D'Youville women seemed to move from moderate Republicanism to support for Roosevelt or perhaps something a bit more radical. The first indicator of problems was a short descriptive piece in the magazine lauding the all class nature of Christmas Eve – Printer's Mass. In 1931 an editorial gently mocked Hoover, but in 1932 an editorial on Hoover's defeat criticized how nasty most U.S. newspapers were to the president at his defeat. The *New York Times* was noted as an exception. The one mention of politics in the interviews of an alumna noted how she remained a Republican to secure a social welfare job (she was trained as a teacher) in Niagara Falls. By 1933, an editorial supported Roosevelt as a great man and in 1934 the debate topic was whether the National Recovery Administration (Roosevelt's program) should be made permanent. In 1935, the class prediction had Huey Long elected president – which would have been a more radical turn. By 1936, a student editorial agreed with critics of Roosevelt's Supreme Court Plan. By then Catholics seemed to have found some more general response to the Depression. In 1937 the magazine reprinted a general text on charity and slightly earlier one of the Oblate Fathers argued for a cooperative movement as an alternative to communism or fascism. In 1939, D'Youville opened a Cooperative Store among the students and created a program to train workers for Cooperatives.[18]

> Like the country as a whole, D'YOUVILLE WOMEN seemed to move from MODERATE REPUBLICANISM to support for Roosevelt or perhaps something a bit more radical.

The 1930s made politics central to all Americans. D'Youville students responded in accordance to their Catholicism and with sympathy to minorities and to those less privileged in society. The college as a college also had to react. As indicated by the mid-1930s the teacher focus was becoming outmoded. Even though the overall figures in 1936 showed many teachers among the graduates in 1937, only eight got teaching positions. More were going on to graduate or other education – four from 1934, eleven by 1938. The administration later tried to bolster teaching by beginning an art education program with the Albright-Knox Gallery, but that attracted few students.[19]

The major new focus in curriculum was to examine society directly. In 1930 Vernon E. Bundy of the *Buffalo News* was hired to create a course in journalism. A few years later sociology – really social work – was initiated in a series of lectures by outside experts that constituted a course on medical sociology. The course included work on public health, public welfare, psychiatric care, etc. By 1937, the Sociology Club sponsored a lecture series on Catholic Charities. Much of this work on sociology was inspired by Sister Mary Imelda who was dean in these years.[20]

The other major new direction was toward business. Business had always been an option at D'Youville, but from the onset of the 1930s it received more emphasis. When Holy Angels Academy separated

59

from the college, some of the space went to typing and shorthand rooms. In 1938, a new club appeared – the Greggorian – for business students. By 1939, thirteen of the fifty-five degrees were in business administration. In 1938 D'Youville also began a free Credit Union School to train Cooperative managers. In the late 1930s, the school also dropped its requirement to graduate from 140 hours of credit to 128 hours. This wider range of options for women in academic life and college training was shared by other women's colleges.[21]

Some aspects of D'Youville changed very little, the most important of which was a tradition of great teaching. The dedications of the yearbook to various sisters, the deep appreciation of Elizabeth Cronyn in the 1920s were part of that tradition. It continued in the 1930s. One name stands out for creating great tension in the classroom – that was Father Kennedy who taught religion and psychology. Students had to think to give answers to his satisfaction. But he is lovingly remembered as are Professor Lappin who taught English from the 1920s through the 1940s, and Sister Saint Ignatius who taught history. The impact of each was visible in the magazine. Lappin's love of Irish literature was reflected in many students' writing critically in that area. He also asked them to examine what a critic does – a whole genre of literature not approached before in the magazine. Most of the sentimental, ironic (in the O'Henry sense) short stories disappeared, replaced by realistic description of daily life, book reviews, etc. Lappin with his connections to Britain helped bring in writers like James Stephens and Lady Sackville West to lecture. He maintained ties to other local institutions and thus Miss Eileen Mulholland came from Buffalo State College to give a preparatory lecture on Stephens. "Dr. Lappin . . . taught us English. He was very good."[22]

Sister Saint Ignatius also had tremendous impact. She organized students to enter an oratorical contest on the role of George Washington in 1932, one of whom won third prize in state competition. These speeches were published in the magazine and Sister Saint Ignatius clearly urged other students to do the same – some thirty-nine articles appeared over the decade compared to a dozen in the previous decade. Jeune Mago remembered, "Sister Ignatius, whom I had for History, was very good," indeed she was her fondest classroom memory. Anna Mae Jones, after naming all three instructors named here (including Father Kennedy) was asked why they were good and she responded, "Because they were interested in you. They always saw that you got what you needed, helped you when you needed it." Not that teaching was always perfect. Asked about fond memories:

> I have many, of all my friends, just being in class, watching the squirrels jump from tree to tree, we had those windows and the great big trees and the squirrels; chemistry class was very boring [laughing].[23]

D'Youville was subtly changing in the 1930s. The students wanted the 1920s to continue, but they couldn't quite afford it. A wonderful small article described looking in stores with no funds – a process titled "Window Wishing" but with no bitterness or resentment involved. Traditions of fine teaching, rich culture, love of the sisters, and feeling for Catholicism continued but toward the end of the decade there was the shift to business – teaching was no longer enough – one had to be practical.[24]

[1] *Statistical History of the U.S.*, Sister Mary Sheila Driscoll, Packet for 75th anniversary; Sally Schwager, "Educating Women in America," *Signs* 12 (Winter 1987), 333-372.

[2] *D'Youvillian*, 1931, p. 143.

[3] *D'Youville Magazine*, 20:3 (1930) p. 54; 19:3 (1930) p. 45; 20:3 (1931) p. 58; 20:4 (1931), p. 5.

[4] *D'Youville Magazine*, 19:3 (1930) p. 44; 22:3 (1933) p. 42. Sister Mary Sheila Driscoll, 1930s and 1940s; *D'Youville Magazine*, 27:4 (1938).

[5] Interview with Anna Mae Jones, D'Youville Oral History Project (in future notes all interviews refer to the oral history project). *D'Youville Magazine*, 22:1 (1932) p. 34. Sister Mary Sheila, 1930s and 1940s. *D'Youville Magazine*, 22:2 (1932) p. 42; 24:4 (1935). Morton and Phyllis Keller, *Making Harvard Modern*. New York, Oxford, 2001, p. 32-46.

[6] *D'Youvillian*, 1931 and 1938; *D'Youville Magazine*, Spring (senior) Issue, 1933-1937; *D'Youville Magazine*, 20:2 (1930) p. 63; 24:1 (1934), p. 35-37.

[7] Interview with Jeune Mago. *D'Youville Magazine*, 20:1 (1930), p. 43; 20:2 (1930), p. 59-60; 23:2 (1933), p. 43-44; 28:2 (1938), p. 28-30; 23:2 (1933) p. 43; 29:1 (1939).

[8] *D'Youville Magazine*, 20:1 (1930) p. 45-47; 25:1 (1935) p. 36-37; 23:3 (1934) p. 45; and 23:4 (1934) p. 43. Interview with Mary Ellen Rowe Maloney.

[9] Interviews with Anna Mae Jones, Jeune Mago, and Mary Ellen Rowe Mahoney.

[10] Ibid., *D'Youville Magazine*, 24:4 (1936) p. 33-38.

[11] Interviews with Jeune Mago Miller, Anna Mae Jones. *D'Youville Magazine*, 22:3 (1933).

[12] *D'Youville Magazine*, 22:4 (1933) p. 61; 25:2 (1935) p. 3.

[13] *D'Youville Magazine*, 20:4 (1931); 24:4 (1935) p. 24; 21:2 (1931); 21:3 (1932) p. 57-58; 23:3 (1934); 26:3 (1937) p. 36-37.

[14] *D'Youville Magazine*, 24:3 (1935) p. 47; 25:2 (1935); 25:3 (1936) p. 42.

[15] *D'Youville Magazine*, 26:1 (1936); 26:3 (1937) p. 34; 27:1 (1937) p. 3-5; 27:4 (1938).

[16] *D'Youville Magazine*, 24:3 (1935); 26:1 (1936); 28:2 (1938); 28.3 (1939); 29:1 (1939).

[17] *D'Youville Magazine*, 24:3 (1935) p. 43; 25.3 (1936); 26.4 (1937); 29.1 (1939).

[18] *D'Youville Magazine*, 20:2 (1931); 20:3 (1931); 22:1 (1932); 23:1 (1933); 24:4 (1934); 24:4 (1935) p. 25; 25:3 (1936) p. 42; 26.2 (1936) p. 42-43; 26:3 (1937); 27:4 (1938); 28.2 (1939). Interview with Mary Ellen Rowe Maloney. Sister Mary Sheila Driscoll, 1930s and 1940s.

[19] *D'Youville Magazine*, 24:3 (1935); 28:1 (1938) p. 24-25; Sister Mary Sheila Driscoll, 1930s and 1940s.

[20] *D'Youville Magazine*, 20:1 (1930) p. 38; 22:1 (1932) p. 37-39; 26:3 (1937) p. 38-9; 28:1 (1938) p. 3-4.

[21] *D'Youville Magazine*, 19:3 (1930) p. 34-37; 27:3 (1934) p. 43; Meeting of the Board of Governors, 1939; Sister Mary Sheila Driscoll, 1930s and 1940s; Susan B. Carter "Academic Women Revisited," *Journal of Social History*, 14 (Summer 1981) p. 75-99.

[22] *D'Youville Magazine*, 1930-39 passim, Sister Mary Sheila Driscoll, 1930s and 1940s. *D'Youville Magazine*, 23:3 (1934); Interview with Jean Mago, Jeune Mago, and Mary Ellen Rowe Maloney.

[23] *D'Youville Magazine*, 21:3 (1932) p. 62 and passim for the decade. Interviews with Jeune Mago and Anna Mae Jones.

[24] *D'Youville Magazine*, 22:2 (1931).

Chapter Four

To War and Back: D'Youville in the 1940s

War raged in the world from the late 1930s but the U.S. and D'Youville remained in an edgy lull. As one D'Youville co-ed put it:

> The despair of trying to look ravishing with thirty competing personalities! These dances and parties were never half as much fun as the preparation for them: everyone be-creamed, be-curled, with witch-hazel pads covering glamorous to be eyes; orchids, gardenias, camellias arriving in familiar, long green boxes. Pre-war days they were, and so unappreciated then! Picnics at Fort Erie offering such carefree pleasures – the hike over and beyond the bridge; the tangle resulting on the opposite side when the variety of birth places were rapidly recited; the unbelieving scowls on more than one official forehead, dissolving into a friendly grin when viewing, and sampling, our plentiful and delicious lunch![1]

While simple pleasures continued, the pre-war period also saw political confusion. Generally the late 1930s saw support for Roosevelt in the *D'Youville Magazine*; in the pre-war 1940s that was challenged on the campus. Already there had been support for Franco. In 1940 the school's International Relations Club affiliated with the Carnegie Foundation to support peace. A little later the students helped sponsor a conference of nine local schools calling for isolationism. These articles were balanced in 1940 by ones seeing Hitler as a barbarian and supporting the British Empire. By 1941, an article saw Germany as the Judas of European culture and saw America as the refuge of art in a barbarian world. There was a plea for American patriotism. Writers in the magazine accepted the need for war preparedness and argued that college students needed to serve.[2]

63

Once the U.S. actually went to war there was full support. The magazine presented stories of war heroism – the push to sell bonds. Editorials appeared on collecting things for the war effort. The young ladies gave blood and trained to do home nursing. In 1942, a peace conference at the school formally adopted Roosevelt's Four Freedoms. The young women at the college actively engaged in selling war bonds, at one point raising the $75,000 needed to pay for and name a pursuit aircraft named, a bit ironically, for the school. Young women took time off from studies to do part-time war work – a description appears in the magazine of a student filling in at a chemical engineering firm.[3]

Class day 1941. Seniors, soon to be graduates. Sophomores held the flowered hoops under which they strolled.

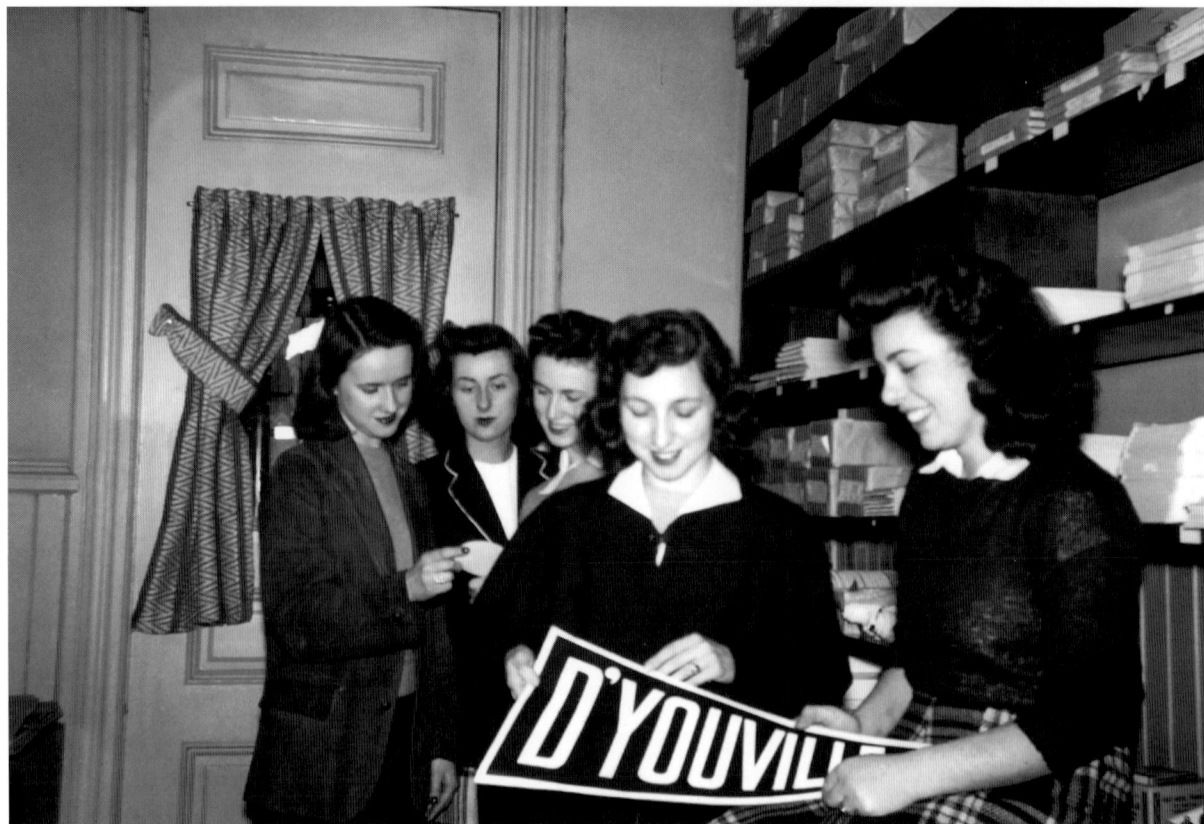

Undergraduates in 1945 getting supplies at the Coop Bookstore. The Coop began in the 1930s as both an economy and as a training program. Notice the one senior, Rita Tropman Walter, in her academic gown.

One alumna interviewed described knitting squares for afghans to be sent to the boys, while attending college assemblies. She also described dances at the University of Buffalo that D'Youville girls attended to be hospitable to the young naval and army personnel stationed at or coming through Buffalo.[4]

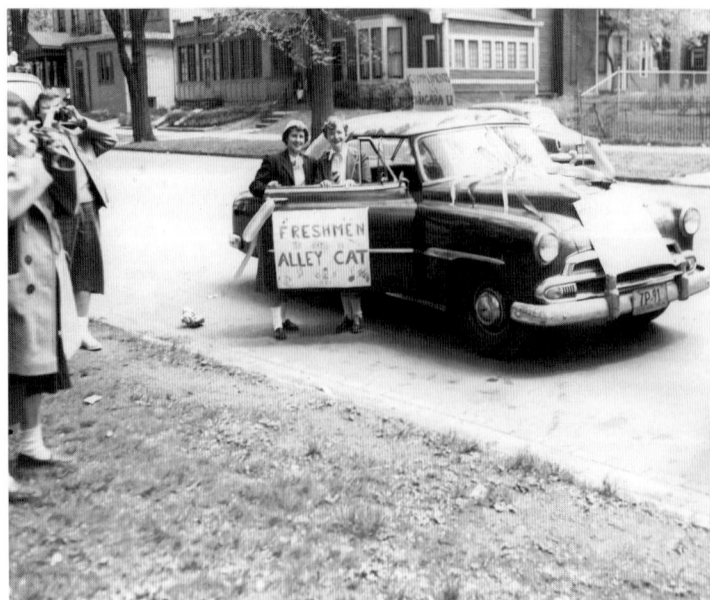

The magazine's alumna section reported that twenty-three D'Youville graduates were engaged in war work, several others joined the Women's Auxiliary Army Corp, another the WAVES (naval equivalent). Three worked for the Red Cross; one, Jane Beckly, trained as a nurse, served with a unit in the North Africa, Italian, and Southern French campaigns. Another alumna served in the consular service

Car decorated for the 1941 Moving Up Day (MUD) Parade. During the war they stopped using cars to save gas.

64

in Lima, Peru. The most illustrious of these graduates was Anne Wood. Already trained as a pilot, she volunteered her services to the British as a pilot to deliver all types of aircraft to the bases where they were needed in England and later in Europe. Some of her letters were reprinted in the magazine, and a fuller report of her activities also appeared toward the end of the war.[5]

The short stories on the war in the magazine depicted bravery and loss, sometimes of the women carrying on at home. The material in the magazine about Wood, the alumni, or personnel activity seemed to say they were doing their part, but this emphasis rather implied their effort was insufficient. The young women seemed to feel they were not doing quite enough. An article in the March 1942 magazine spoke of the war but commented that life on campus went on as usual. Actually, this was not quite true since the reported college activities dropped from a mean of eighteen or nineteen per graduate to a low of eleven for the class of 1944. Contrast between support for the war and limited ability to affect it can be seen in two yearbook dedications. In 1943, the yearbook was dedicated to Emily Dickinson:

> Our spirits should soar skyward on the wings of American patriotism, enabling our speech and our acts, so that we strengthen our own morale but also lead others onto the part of Americanism. Emily Dickinson was noted as the embodiment of womanliness, Americanism and courage.[6]

The same year the *D'Youvillian* commented on the prom, "A uniform was a common sight that night – and we all knew that many a smiling face concealed an aching heart." By 1944, the elaborate parade of cars that symbolized Moving Up Day had to be abandoned, but the event still took place. The students skated or marched "while our lovely queen and her charming attendants drove at our head in a quaint barouche." The dedication in 1946 was to their brothers:

> In leaving D'Youville, we pause to render thanks to those who kept the war from engulfing our college education, and who won the victory, which enables us to enter a world at peace. As an expression of our gratitude we dedicate this yearbook to our brothers. The book itself is a souvenir of years spent in quiet happy hours of higher education which so many brothers preserved for us by their own sacrifice.[7]

One alumna put this all quite poignantly:

> Well, we were very nervous . . . during the war. So there was a very, I want to say, religious feeling, we were concerned for the people who were suffering or dying. It was rough and we spent a lot of time in the chapel and a lot of time with the chaplain. It was a rough time for us, really, because we were young and our emotions, our young men were over there and a lot were dying over there or coming home hurt and we were praying for them all the time.

A contemporary comment in the same vein from the *D'Youville Magazine* read:

> Perpetually burning vigil lights before our Lady's Shrine in the Chapel. Slow moving Rosaries in slim, young hands. Bowed heads whispering fervent prayers for a soldier's safe return.[8]

65

In 1940 two students, Jeanne Burke and Blanch Kechoel, joined the MUD parade on an old tandem dressed in the appropriate attire for 1912. A copy of this picture hangs in the college center vestibule. (Many had thought it dated to 1912 and some thought it peculiar since it looks political and the students were distinctly not political in 1912, Ruth Kelly noted the hair was not proper for 1912.)

D'YOUVILLE CLASS OF 1912

Sentiment and politics were not the only effect of the war upon D'Youville College. Men went to war, even Harvard temporarily admitted women to some programs during the war. Male faculty at the college could not be replaced. Women on the faculty rose from 84% (48% were sisters) in 1940, to 93% (55% were sisters) in 1945. Because eight of the Grey Nuns had PhDs the ratio of the PhDs on the faculty went to 28% in 1945.[9]

While the war never threatened the survival of D'Youville College – it was insulated by the support of the Grey Nuns who taught a majority of the classes – the number of students did drop significantly in the early 1940s. In 1941, only fifty-seven freshmen

> Well, we were very nervous . . . during the war. So there was a very, I want to say, RELIGIOUS FEELING, we were concerned for the people who were SUFFERING or dying.

entered, compared with seventy-three the year before. That class of seventh-three dwindled to sixty-one (plus eleven sisters) by graduation in 1943. The early 1940s saw the number pictured in the yearbook drop from 275 in 1940 to 235 in 1944 and 1945. The number of sisters who attended did rise over these years (and they were never pictured). The insecurity about enrollment drove innovation in programming. A special program for sisters was created where they studied full-time in college for several years (some joined then as well) and then worked as teachers in various Grey Nun schools. They returned to finish their degree in a special summer program. The number of graduates in this program rose from one in 1943 to fourteen in 1948. Some sisters graduated in the regular program as well. Another innovation was to accelerate the four years of college into three by using the summer period and appending classes during the year. As the *D'Youvillian* commented:

> To accelerating students – our blessing . . . our feeble minds only become more confused
> when we attempt to figure out the whys and wherefores of your schedules and classes.[10]

Innovation from the 1930s continued, particularly the program leading to a BS in commerce. Thirty-two of the graduates (of eighty-four) took this degree in 1944. The most significant change was the introduction of a nursing major in 1942. Planning for the major began in the 1930s. Nursing was a small profession. There were only seventy baccalaureate programs in 1936 and 1,472 hospital programs. Hospitals were the primary employer of nurses – they received some support from the federal government in the 1930s. With the war, D'Youville qualified for federal aid to establish its program. Sister Saint Rosalie, GNSH, RN, who held a BS and an MA in nursing education from Catholic University, was the first director. The great concern of the students was that they would be "armchair nurses." The program included a summer in Ogdensburg, New York, after their freshman and sophomore years and clinical rotations in the Buffalo area at Mount Saint Mary's (general), Children's Hospital, Mount Morris Hospital (tuberculosis), and Buffalo State Hospital (psychiatric) in their junior and senior years.

67

Joan Robinson (center) and friends at MUD in 1945. Ms. Robinson later taught at the college; volunteered as an instructor at Christ the King Seminary; and served on the SUNY at Buffalo advisory board. She died in a bizarre accident and was remembered by students at the college in a yearbook dedication in 1993.

68

Margaret Curry (who later joined the D'Youville faculty and was a member of the first class of seven) noted:

> We went to the country. None of us had ever been away from home, and we were used to having our summers off . . . It was exciting though, because we actually got in and took care of patients . . . We had a time to go to bed, a time to get up. We had to go to Mass every morning before we went on duty. It was like being in the Army!

She also remembered Mother Saint Rosalie as a "very kind, interesting person. She was interested in our experience, so we had a lot of close contact with her."[11]

The nursing classes remained small throughout the 1940s. They were supplemented by a hospital and medical technology degree which had its first graduate in 1946. The 1940s saw D'Youville firmly launched toward training for medical specialties which would be part of the continuing heritage.

But the school also remained a small traditional liberal arts school. In 1949, the second largest major among graduates was English. Even the BS in commerce with twenty-eight majors had nineteen of that major completing an education concentration. Teaching, therefore, remained the focus of many of the students. One alumna indicated this feeling of a broad education:

> I enjoyed it because I took everything I wanted. We didn't work outside of the college at that time, so I think we could do more. But I remember doing all the sciences and maths, plus Latin, French, all the humanities. And I wrote for the English journal that we put out. It was a journal of articles and poetry. I wish I now had time to write poetry. We had access to so many opportunities. I had enough credits to major in anything. I had my choice, a wide choice.[12]

This alumna eventually completed a mathematics major.

The college also recruited in a traditional manner. Of the graduates of 1949, 46% had come from Buffalo area Catholic high schools and eighteen of this 46% came from Holy Angels Academy. In the small classes recruited early in the war – 1946 graduates – these figures had risen to 66% and 24%, respectively.

In 1945, an article in the *D'Youville Magazine* attacked a broad criterion of American higher education by Malcolm Cowley which charged soulless indifference. The article quoted Sister Mary of the Visitation:

> The primary motivation of education is not the acquisition of knowledge, but to use knowledge in the pursuit of life's ideals, which to Christians, is an ultimate union with God.

The article also attacked the idea that indifference was a model at D'Youville:

> There is not one teacher who is not vitally alive, active, and enthusiastic. Each one is eager to guide and direct us, not only in his field, but in life itself. They are our friends, as easily approached as a school mate, both during class and after.[13]

Another alumna who later joined the order put the "he" in the above quote in its proper female perspective:

> We knew them all . . . my heavens, we lived with them . . . When they finished teaching we went over and they lived in the same building that we lived in so we had a lot of interaction with them. They were good to us I have to say . . . the young Sisters.[14]

69

This close affinity to Catholicism continued through the 1940s. Sister Rosalie Bertell remembered that during the Korean War the students said a constant rosary in a room off the chapel.[15]

The Catholicism that was part of the tradition of the school also helped bring D'Youville into the mainstream American culture in the later 1940s, first in terms of the conservative issue of anti-communism and comment on foreign policy, and second in terms of the struggles for inclusion of

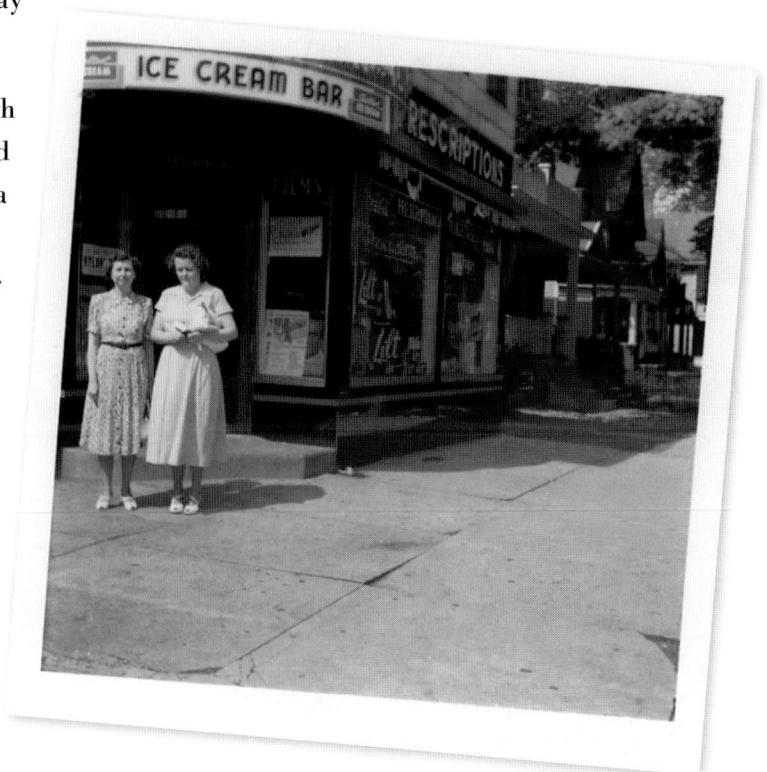

The College Pharm located just past Holy Angels Church at West and York Streets was a popular spot to get a short distance off campus and have a soda. The photo is from the1940s; the building still exists but has long been closed.

Students going to class in the late 1940s on the west staircase of the Prospect building. Students weren't allowed on the central staircase.

The class of 1947 with their retreat master. Each class had a religious retreat every year during the first five decades of the college.

Sister Francis Xavier teaching a chemistry lab to Sister Mary Leo, a student in 1945. Sister Francis Xavier became the head of nursing and later one of the dynamic builders of the campus when she served as president.

all Americans. While Roosevelt was praised for establishing the Peace Conference in 1945, he was criticized for Yalta, for pre-war diplomatic activity, and for spending $2 billion on the atomic bomb. Actually, this was a call to spend similar amounts on social issues. In later years, Orwell's *Animal Farm* was positively reviewed as was Mauriac's description of the Warsaw uprising and slaughter. In 1949, Cardinal Mindzenty was praised for his struggles against communism in Hungary.[16]

Positive attitudes toward a broader definition of Americanism were always part of the American Catholic Church. Catholics were not a mainstream group in the nineteenth and early twentieth centuries. D'Youville and the preceding Holy Angels Academy had always been open to others, but there were few non-Catholics and very few non-Caucasian women. Inclusion became a greater emphasis after World War II. As the war ended, the *D'Youville Magazine* published an editorial on the Pope's Peace Plan of 1937 which had called for greater toleration of ethnic and racial differences. The next year, a long article appeared on why prejudice is a learned cultural behavior. In 1947, the magazine reviewed material condemning prejudice and in 1949 a review appeared on the negative effects of racial segregation in the Army – a clear support of President Truman's order to end such discrimination. More significantly, Ethel Kregg, clearly an ordinary African American, was pictured among the sophomores in the yearbook. In the same year, Cecilia Grace Fong from Hong Kong, was the first foreign student to graduate.[17]

Student attitudes at the college could be both conservative and reflect the changing ideas of the later '40s. One former nursing student remembered literally marching from class to class, as a group, in silence. Another disputed this and said it might have been true of the nursing students who had a very rigid program, but certainly not of anyone else. Indeed, she recalled leading a small rebellion in student government. The specific campaign she led was a struggle that took place twenty years before in many colleges:

> My crusade was to get the smoker rooms, and later I became a cancer research scientist and was horrified at what I had done. But we had the lunch room in the basement, in the school part, was one smoke room and the other was the kitchenette, on the fourth floor. Smoke rooms, that was the big human rights thing we did.

Students not only struggled for some rights (even ones now found ironic), but they also reached out beyond Catholic institutions. In the late 1940s, D'Youville students belonged not just to the National Federation of Catholic College Students, but also to the National Student Association

The chemistry lab in 1945. It had changed very little over the decades from the opening of the college.

73

Mothers and alumnae gather in 1943 for a formal tea. These formal afternoons were a continuing part of the college routine through the 1950s. ———

74

These young ladies were dressed for the 1949 boarders Christmas party. In the 1940s relatively few could board at the college since it had almost no space. ————————

(these organizations had split in the 1930s over the question of Franco and Spain).[18]

As the economy picked up with the war, D'Youville alumnae married. The magazine reported eight marriages in the spring issue of 1941 and another fourteen in the fall of 1941. In the fall of 1942 a short story depicted a young woman saved by the burning touch of her Saint Mary's medal when she planned to elope and marry outside the church. Even at the height of the war, when the alumnae section was reporting all sorts of war work, six marriages were noted. A senior reflection in May of 1944 recalled "exquisite diamonds being slipped on third fingers at Christmas and Easter." In 1949, the governor's book noted that the college was running two Pre-Cana classes to meet the needs of graduates who would be marrying. D'Youville women were preparing to be part of the coming baby boom.[19]

While the enrollment at D'Youville had recovered by 1949 – the school graduated 107 that year and the yearbook pictured 324 with 95 freshmen – these numbers paled at

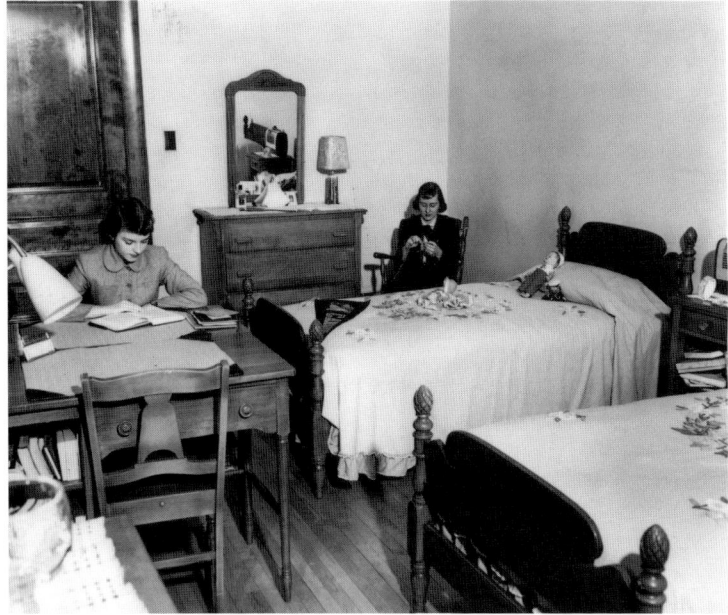

This was a typical dorm room on the fourth floor of the old building in the 1940s. This space is now devoted to the Learning Center.

A piano/violin duet being practiced in 1940, part of the rich musical tradition of the early decades.

what happened in higher education generally. The late 1940s were the years of the GI Bill. Veterans flocked to campuses, beginning the trend toward mass higher education. The male/female ratio of college students swung decidedly in favor of males and would remain so for several decades. Women's colleges like D'Youville tried to help balance this ratio, but without substantial growth they would not. Their small size meant that most students, male or female, would experience higher education at larger state institutions. The growth of these institutions was phenomenal in the late 1940s and after. D'Youville would grow in the 1950s and that growth would reflect continued societal needs in education and the medical fields, but it would also have problems of its own. After the 1940s, D'Youville was on a roller coaster ride.

75

[1] *D'Youville Magazine*, 33:4 (May 1944) p. 5-6.

[2] *D'Youville Magazine*, 29:3 (November 1940); 30:1 (February 1941) p. 32-33; 30:1 (February 1941); 30:3 (November 1941).

[3] *D'Youville Magazine*, 31:3 (November 1942); 31:4 (December 1942); 32:1 (February 1943); 32:3 (November 1943); 32:4 (December 1943); 34:2 (June 1944); *D'Youvillian*, 1944, p. 43.

[4] Interview with Mrs. Bauer.

[5] *D'Youville Magazine*, 32:2 (June 1942); 34:4 (December 1944); 34:2 (June 1944); 34:1 (February 1944); 32:1 (February 1942); 34:2 (June 1944).

[6] *D'Youville Magazine*, 31:1 (March 1942). *D'Youvillian*, 1940, 1941, 1942, 1943, 1944, 1945, 1946, 1947. *D'Youvillian*, 1943.

[7] *D'Youvillian*, 1943, p. 48; *D'Youvillian*, 1941 and 1944, p. 42; *D'Youvillian*, 1946, p. 7.

[8] Interview with Jean Mago. *D'Youville Magazine*, 33:4 (May 1944), p. 13.

[9] Morton and Kelly, *Making Harvard Modern*, p. 47-63. *D'Youvillian*, 1940-1945.

[10] *D'Youvillian*, 1943, p. 40. Board of Governors Book, D'Youville Archives. *D'Youvillian*, 1940-1946.

[11] Board of Governors Book, D'Youville Archives. Janice Cooke Feigenbaum, "History of the Division of Nursing of D'Youville College, 1942-1992." Typescript, D'Youville Archives.

[12] *D'Youvillian*, 1949; Interview with Sister Rosalie Bertell.

[13] *D'Youville Magazine*, 34:4 (December 1945), p. 25 and 27. *D'Youvillian*, 1940-1949, particularly 1946 and 1949.

[14] Interview with Sister Mary O'Connell.

[15] Interview with Sister Rosalie Bertell.

[16] *D'Youville Magazine*, 34:4 (December 1945); 34:3 (November 1945); 35:1 (March 1946); 35:4 (December 1946); 36:3 (November 1947); 39:1 (March 1950).

[17] *D'Youville Magazine*, 34:3 (November 1945); 35:4 (December 1946); 36:3 (November 1947); 39:1 (November 1949). *D'Youvillian*, 1949, p. 24.

[18] Interview with Sister Rosalie Bertell; *D'Youvillian*, 1949.

[19] *D'Youville Magazine*, 30:4 (May 1941), p. 39-40; 31:1 (November 1941), p. 41; 32:1 (November 1942); 34:4 (June 1945); 33:4 (May 1944), p. 14. Board of Governors Book, 1949, D'Youville Archives.

Chapter Five

Happy Days at D'Youville

America had won the war – it led the world in reconstruction and a rising tide of economic well being. Nuclear weapons and a nasty competition with the Soviet Union clouded the horizon, but America responded by smoothing out recessions, stalwartly facing the threat of communism, and busily seeking new wonders and technologies. In this era, most folks had a car. Ordinary folks began to fly about the country, many were moving to the suburbs, and everyone began to watch television. Such marvels needed educated men, and the GI Bill of the 1940s created mass education for men. By the 1950s, despite a drop in the age of marriage (and a subsequent baby boom) women began to seek equal education opportunities. The GI Bill and the growth of large state universities brought on a previous gender ratio of 41% female BA, BS graduates (when few went to college), to a new low with women being only 24% of BA and BS graduates in 1950 (with 432,000 such degrees being awarded). Toward the end of the 1950s, while numbers had not grown very much, the ratio of women was over 34%. Much of the growth of women's education in the 1950s and well into the 1960s took place at Catholic women's colleges. At its peak, in 1968, there were 101,000 such students at 142 Catholic women's colleges (about one of every four students in the country).[1]

The Grey Nun faculty (still almost half the faculty) try to find their places to march in to graduation in 1956.

78

D'Youville shared in this growth; student population rose from just short of four hundred in 1950, to seven hundred in 1960. Tuition also rose from $300 a year to $650 in the decade. The number of students graduating did not rise as quickly – basically 120 graduated in 1950 and did so again in 1960. By 1966, that number reached 163. As stated in a 1952 study for re-accreditation, the most immediate need was space for the library. The crowding and the suburbanization of Buffalo drove the college administrators to consider moving the college to a new site. Canisius tentatively offered space next to their campus with the long-run aim of creating a joint institution. The Canisius offer was rejected and a whole new site looked prohibitively expensive, so a fund drive began in 1954 for a new library building. The college broke ground on the new library in 1955 and it opened the next year. It was located just to the north of the Prospect wing of the old building on Prospect Avenue, on former tennis courts. In 1955, the college laid out a master plan including ten new buildings, and they purchased an old apartment house, six or seven blocks from the college, for dormitory use (it was used until 1966). In 1958-59, Madonna Hall, a residence, dining, and community hall, was completed. The building attached to the east end of the original building. The site was formerly a grassy play area with outdoor basketball nets.[2]

The 1950 graduation class aligned behind the bishop at Kleinhans Hall. The bishop at this time still served as chancellor of the college and officially awarded degrees.

The glories of HOLY ANGELS CHURCH during a baccalaureate Mass in the 1950s. Baccalaureate services remain popular among faculty and some students to this day.

The college always had dormitory space in the upper reaches of the original building, but only a few could reside. D'Youville remained both a local and a commuter school in the 1950s. In 1950, 59% of the graduates were from the city of Buffalo, 20% from suburbs, and 7% from western New York. Only 11%—twelve young women—had to board. In 1959, the figures of seniors had changed little: 52% of the young women were from the city, 23% from suburbs, and 9% from western New York. Only eighteen of the young women (or 16%) had to board. The apartment house had space for twenty-four young women and Madonna Hall, the new dormitory, had about sixty rooms set up for double occupancy. Maximum dormitory space was 150, but enrollment in 1960 was over 700. Some of the space was clearly occupied by the students from Buffalo or its suburbs who wished and could afford to get away from home.[3]

The Grey Nuns present small gifts to the seniors in the 1950s. This was a formal occasion—note the white glove grasped in a senior's hand.

82

In the 1950s, the nursing program became its own school in the college, and in 1951, Sister Francis Xavier became dean. One student remembered her from an entrance interview as very charismatic, elegant, and inspiring. A young faculty member and graduate, Margaret Curry, called her "very forward thinking, an organizational person who got us all involved in the League and the District" and "kept pushing us to go for graduate school."

She could also be warmly sympathetic. Once when Buffalo State Hospital refused to let student nurses attend Christmas Mass, she grabbed a cab, dressed in full habit, and came to intervene. One of the senior nursing students expected (and got) a marriage proposal at that Mass.

By 1950, New York State and all other states agreed to a combined nursing license examination and D'Youville

Class day remained a popular time in 1952. Formal dresses, lots of flowers, tradition deep seated, but about to end.

MUD parades grew larger in the 1950s. The junior class did this queen's court float in 1953.

nurses could be licensed by passing the exams in all states. In 1956-57, the National League of Nursing granted temporary accreditation to the program. In the 1952 report to Middle States Accrediting Association, D'Youville showed ninety-four students enrolled in the major. In 1958, they added a program to allow hospital-trained nurses to get a baccalaureate degree. Nursing degrees became more necessary as the profession was oriented to hospital work (with nurses acting as supervisors to nurses' aides, etc.) and the Korean War created shortages. The college's orientation to medical areas was also apparent in the graduation of seven hospital technicians and eight medical secretaries in 1955.[4]

While nursing and medical studies added numbers to the college, its traditional strengths in education did not diminish. With the post-war baby boom and growth of the suburbs, the Diocese of Buffalo suffered a severe teacher shortage. In 1951, D'Youville began a Cadet Teacher core to fill this need. Young women received tuition from the diocese in exchange for teaching half the year (the other half and summers were spent at D'Youville getting more thoroughly qualified and better educated). Those enrolled committed themselves for four years and three summers to receiving a full baccalaureate degree. In the late 1950s, the state allowed D'Youville to grant education degrees for elementary and primary school teachers. In the 1930s and 1940s, business degrees had been popular, but while the degree continued into the 1950s, it also became tied to education. Of thirty-seven business degrees

An elaborate procession of cars in 1958.

85

in 1950, twenty-eight included an education track. By the end of the decade, there were only seven such degrees with six tied to education. Between business education and the traditional secondary education tied to a liberal arts major, sixty-seven of the graduates in 1950 were headed to teaching (vs. eleven nurses graduating). By 1959, there were thirty-one graduates in all forms of education and thirty-three nurse graduates.

The other strong and innovative program at the college was a solid presence in sociology with students aimed for social work and a number of economics majors whom Reverend Healy, "the labor priest," was preparing for careers in industrial relations. Seven young women graduated in these fields in 1950, and twelve did so in 1959.[5]

For the 1952 Middle States Report, the college studied its alumnae. This report, near the half century mark for the college, showed its traditions and strengths. About half of all graduates since 1912 had married – very few had divorced. Eight percent had entered religious orders and 1.5% had died. The other 40.5% were single women in professional careers. Almost half (49.1%) were in teaching, educational administration, or libraries. About 20% of all graduates were in business. Social work or counseling claimed 12.3%. Only 3% were nurses, with another 4.6% in medical endeavors, and 2.2% were in scientific work. The quality of the early graduates was shown by 68% going on to advanced degrees. They obviously followed earlier patterns by devoting themselves to careers and not marrying. The continued quality of D'Youville's programs was established by 20% of the graduates of 1940-46 having completed graduate degrees.[6]

While programs changed slowly, so did the teaching faculty of the college. In 1950, the balance remained with religious faculty: twenty-one sisters, one priest, three lay men, and twelve lay women. (Women were almost 90% of the faculty.) By 1959, there were only seventeen sisters, three priests, five lay men, and twenty lay women. The college had hired ten new faculty. The gender ratio was now a little under 80% women and lay faculty slightly out numbered those with religious vows. In the 1952 report, the college said ten of the faculty of forty-two had doctorates and twenty had master's degrees. (Eight faculty only had bachelor's degrees and four had special degrees – one French license which would be more than an MA). Seven of those doctorates were held by sisters and almost all the rest of the sisters held master's degrees. Middle States was mildly critical of the college for too few doctorates. That problem was not addressed by 1959; the number had slipped to eight, of which five were held by sisters. Middle States suggested in a reply to a progress report in 1959 that the problem might lie with very low salaries: professors made from $3600 to $4000. (Assistant professors at state universities averaged $5000 in 1950 – two steps lower and 20% more.)[7]

Dr. Joseph Grande, who came in 1958 for what he thought would be a few years – he didn't like the salary – but stayed for thirty-seven years, commented on teaching:

Programs sometimes decorated cars for the MUD parade. The Med Tech groups work on a car in 1952.

Caroling at the Student Government Christmas party in the 1950s which showed music tradition remained viable.

87

The best things were the students . . . I really enjoyed them. They were committed, they were bright, etc. . . . As far as teaching was concerned, nobody bothered you or was breathing down your back at all, [even] though it was obviously a Catholic girls' college until 1971. There wasn't any monitoring . . . it was great. And there was camaraderie because there were a lot of nuns who were teaching there at the time, but there was a core of lay people and we sort of developed a very close relationship.

Later he added:

The core also included some of the nuns . . . they were real live wires. We had a great time . . . They were . . . really down to earth. Some of the sisters were more conservative and traditional and there were the younger ones that were beginning to move out of that old, very conservative atmosphere.

Since sisters were the administrators, he also commented on that aspect of the position:

I sat on a number of committees. One of the committees . . . was the attendance committee. That was an experience. Sister Marie Christine [Dean of Academic Affairs] was the Chair there. And one of the students was a sophomore by the name of Rita Margraff, who later became a Grey Nun . . .

And Margaret Curry who of course was on the nursing faculty for many years . . . [You would ask why are you coming] in late and some of the girls would be very frank and say there were biological reasons why they were sick or something . . . For a guy who was one of the few men in a girls' college, that was pretty hard for me to take.

He also gave a further picture of working with some of the sisters:

Then I sat on some other academic committees where you had some of the real power houses . . . Sister Irene Marie was basically a dean [of business] . . . the chairman of the English Department was Sister [Sr. Mary Geraldine Byrne] . . . Sister Francis Xavier was dean of nursing . . . you saw the interplay between them in terms of the rivalries and stuff like that. I just sat and watched it. But it was interesting . . . They were just like anybody else.

If D'Youville was subtly changing it was not very apparent to the students. Tradition remained strong and had a strong Catholic emphasis. The yearbook dedication of the 1950s included the Grey Nuns (twice) and Marguerite D'Youville (once), Pope Pius XII, the Sacred Heart of Jesus, and D'Youville College and specifically the alumnae for maintaining their traditions. Grande noted about tradition:

I mean I'd go into class and they'd all stand up, and then they'd wait until we said a prayer . . . When they left class, they backed up; they'd never turn their back on me. When you walked down the staircase, if they saw you coming, they all stopped and got over to the side and let you go through. It was a very different world than it was at Notre Dame . . . The first time I walked down the staircase and they all stopped . . . I didn't know what was wrong . . . I was dumbfounded.[8]

The Middle States inspectors commented on:

The deep sense of religious awareness, the courtesy of these girls who have been in contact with these generous, thoughtful, kindly women, who are their instructors and leaders, and the whole attitude of eager anticipation, which they bring to their duties, are all evidence of the character-building influence at work among them.[9]

An alumna remembers the atmosphere in a similar fashion:

You just felt a part of it. Maybe it was the personality of the institution, but you never felt like an outsider and [that] you had to try something to fit in. You automatically began [as] part of the freshman class and that was it. There wasn't any high brow, low brow; we were all one. I think we were all scratching our heads feeling how did I make it to college?

Even though you were in a smaller place, there was no fooling around. We had a good time, but it was in the context that you were learning . . . You were there to learn and they were there to teach you. It was a perfect fit.[10]

The students expressed conservative and Catholic attitudes in the *D'Youville Magazine* which was published through the 1950s (although for a few years they called it *The Muse*). On academic subjects,

In 1954 (and throughout the 1950s) the young ladies' dates for the prom met with the Grey Nuns at a pre-prom reception. Joseph Grande recalls this as being intimidating; it was certainly in loco parentis written large. ————————

89

New programs were begun in the 1950s. In this photo a group of Grey Nuns return for summer school to finish their degrees having taught in the Catholic school system during the year. ————

The first cadet program graduates in 1955. These young women had alternated semesters in class with teaching in schools of the diocese. The diocese paid for their education—another innovative program of the decade.

they published editorials defending teaching classics, teaching rhetoric, and praising the fact they had to take two hours of religion and four more hours of scholastic philosophy. One editorial attacked the materialism of the 1950s:

> We hear the cries of the dispirited, dehumanized beings who are minds without hearts, bodies without souls. We feel the anxiety and desperation of those who are caught in a sterile maze of material progress.

The issue in November of 1954 specifically defended Catholic education which it saw as being criticized for producing "Papist mannequins." Echoing the words of Newman and Jacques Maritain, the editorial saw Catholic education as follows:

> His education must fit him not only to earn a living but also to learn the value of living. He must be able to meet any of the situations of the world . . . His education should never stop.[11]

Students also wrote about specific Catholic and political issues. Their editorials attacked birth control and communism in the same few paragraphs. The Canadian Broadcast System was questioned for allowing Planned Parenthood to appear. A story pointed out the tragedy of divorce.

The first new building erected in the 1950s was a library.
Students crowd the reading room in 1956.

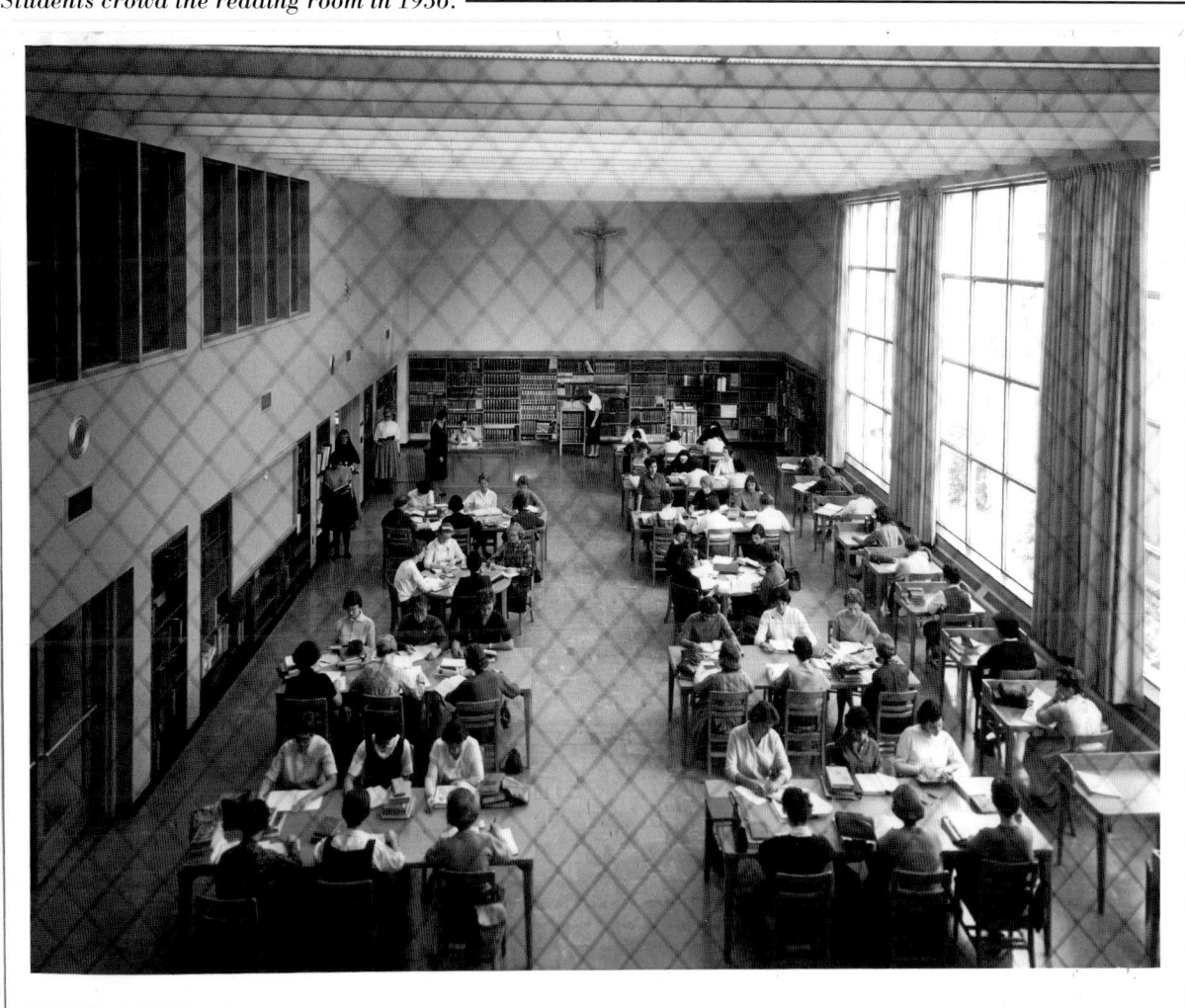

D'Youville was proud to be part of the Marian year in 1955. About 40% of the book reviews the students printed dealt with religious works, from tales of conversion to the great works of Thomas Merton. Graham Greene was also a favorite. *The Nun's Story* was not appreciated.[12]

Like the rest of America, D'Youville young women took part in anti-communism. Some of this came from the instructors. "Sister Grace, when we had her she had been president of the college but we had her when we were in [history] and she was always talking about communism." Another such instructor was Antanas Musteikis:

> He had lived in, he was a Lithuanian, he had fled when the Russians tried to destroy Lithuanian culture . . . He was very anti-communist obviously . . . Tony was involved in different groups [and] he picketed. I remember I was involved in the Council on World Affairs and we sponsored a Soviet educational exhibition downtown and he was out there with all the Lithuanians and the Latvians and the Hungarians, marching, demonstrating against the exhibition.[13]

Students presented these positions in the *D'Youville Magazine*. There was an attack on the Yalta settlement in 1951. The "police action" nature of the Korean struggle was criticized. In 1958, a vignette appeared on the Brussels World Fair comparing unfavorably the Soviet pavilion to that of Vatican City. In the next issue, Sister Jeanette Bauer attacked the communist regime in Romania. In 1959, Khrushchev and his antics were compared to the dignity of a visit to Fatima. The students in the journal primarily looked at literature, church culture, so these concerns were not primary. A review of a lecture at Niagara University in 1956 warned that communism could happen here. The views found in spy novels and more solid critiques like Arthur Koestler's *Darkness at Noon* also appeared.[14]

While D'Youville young women were of their time and place, they could and did appreciate some criticism of the 1950s as already noted in terms of materialism. In the same vein, Sloan Wilson's *Man in a Gray Flannel Suit* and John Galbraith's *Affluent Society* got positive reviews in the magazine. The young women also appreciated modern currents in poetry and T. S. Eliot was particularly well reviewed. Even James Joyce's *The Dubliners* received praise, a reversal from earlier decades. Students, however, were not quite

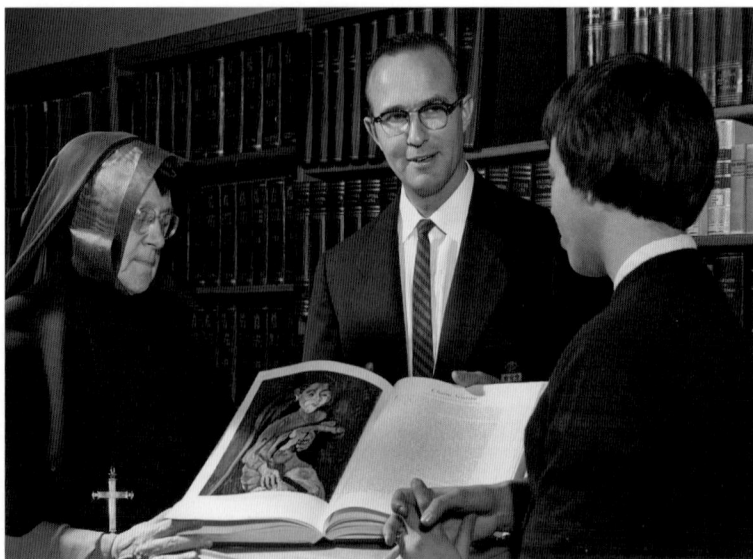

Larry Griffiths, a prominent local sculptor and then faculty member, poses in the new library with Sister Saint Ruth, D'Youville's librarian from 1931 to 1961.

The roll-out stacks of the library which never worked very well since the books were difficult to find. ─────

Typical dorm room in Madonna in 1959. The space was later converted into offices and now houses DaVinci High School. ─────

Kim Young Soon, a Korean student in 1959, showed the college was moving toward a more diverse future.

94

clear on how to evaluate Albert Camus's *The Plague.*[15]

Also continuing from the previous decade was a positive attitude toward racial integration and a sympathy for the question of race. Two short stories appeared in the *D'Youville Magazine* in 1953 and 1954: one was the story of a young woman who became a nun to overcome racial barriers, the other was the portrait of a beautiful toddler, who charms the neighborhood, including the postman who calls her his Portuguese beauty, only to go to school and face the ugliness of the word "nigger." Throughout the 1950s, African American faces appeared in the yearbook. There was also one African American as well as two foreign students (from China and Korea) who graduated.[16]

Students became aware of trying to overcome racial barriers in a still racial society. A student remembered being forced to stay at the college for Thanksgiving break. She and another out-of-town friend wanted to go to the Katherine Lawrence, a fine restaurant in the Wilcox Mansion (where Theodore Roosevelt had been sworn into office, now a museum).

> There was one other student who had stayed, she was from Albany, she was black. And I remember our wanting to invite her to go out to dinner with us, but not knowing where we could go that wouldn't be an uncomfortable situation for her because we were two white students and a black student . . . it was before the civil rights movement and . . . we just were uneasy as to how she might be accepted. So I know we asked her but I think she declined.[17]

Generally, the level of student activity remained high. All the clubs affiliated with majors continued (although sometimes combined, like a Modern Language Club). Ninety young women sang in the Glee Club (about one in seven). Residents kept particularly busy with fall and spring picnics, a residents' dance (held at a downtown hotel), the traditional Halloween party, two formal dinners, and several formal teas through the year. The sisters had help in moderating these and other college activities. For example, a dean's committee checked attendance at assemblies "trying with a measure of success to determine which twin was missing." A maintenance committee kept order in dining areas making sure trays were returned, etc. The college sponsored four other formal dances: the yearbook dance, Knight's dance, sophomore dance, and the junior prom. Grande remembered dating a girl from D'Youville in

1956 and attending the prom, but first there was a reception at the college. "We had to be all dressed up. It was scary seeing this line of nuns. You had to go through the line and shake their hands. That was before the dances down at the Statler."[18]

Dances were a major social activity. While the college sponsored several, the young women were in demand elsewhere as well.

> Once a month, they would have dances. Actually, I think it was twice a month. We used to take buses on Friday nights to Canisius, Niagara University, and St. Bonaventure University. That was fun because it was a two hour drive. We would start maybe [on] Friday at five and get there at seven. The dance would be at seven and lasted until eleven. Then we had to find our way home. Now remember, the [city] buses only ran up to a certain time, so we had to get our parents from North Tonawanda to come to school to take us home.[19]

While the dances were well remembered, this was when Moving Up Day reached fairly dramatic heights. Margraff described building floats:

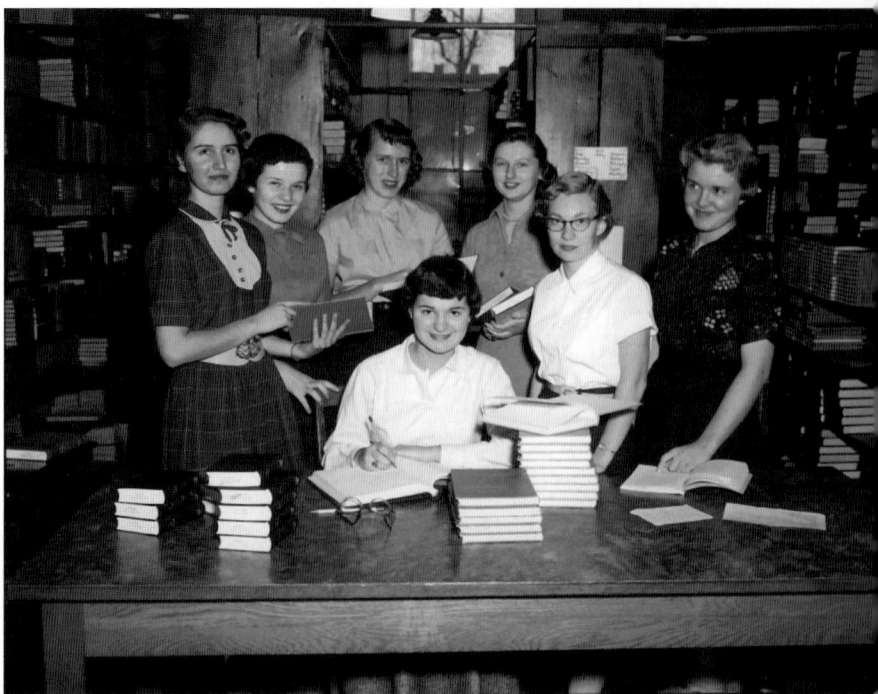

96

The bookroom which rented texts to students remained into the 1950s. The practice certainly reduced costs to the students, but book content began to change more rapidly so the custom was not feasible.

Business subjects came to the college in the 1930s. In 1954 Sister Joseph instructs a typing class.

Each floor in Madonna has its own snack and cooking area. Notice the ashtray on the table, smoking was still allowed, at least in the lounge.

Oh, at least four or five . . . then cars would be decorated and there would be a queen . . . and she had a court and she'd be on the senior float . . .

They usually had a theme and they were [on] a big flatbed truck and then the whole side of this thing, you would have chicken wire and you would make flowers out of tissues, different colors . . . it might have something written in there . . . [they were built] in the Armory on Connecticut . . . and we could only stay out till 11:00, so what we would do is go back to the dorms and make flowers and some day-student would come to the dorm and get our flowers and take them back.

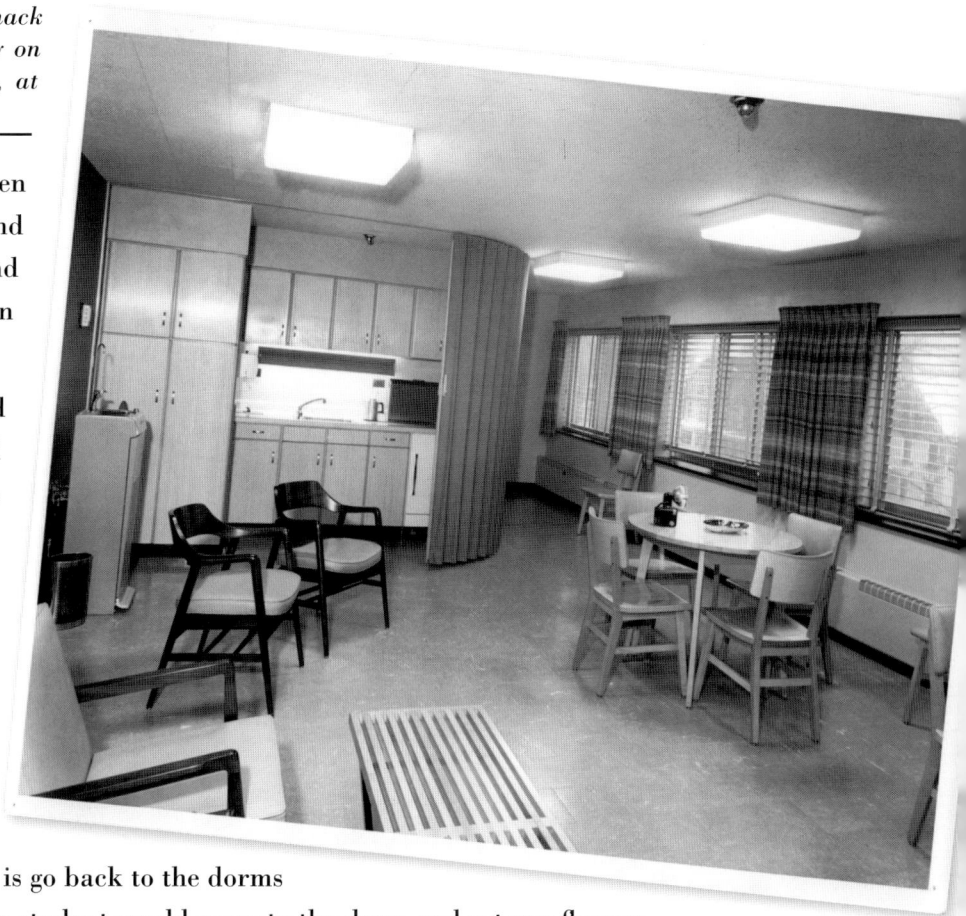

Another alumna noted:

I forgot the theme of it but we got a horse . . . it was a display horse. We got it from Hengerer's. A friend of ours [worked] at Hengerer's and we borrowed this horse. Anyway, because of the rocking and stuff this poor horse keeled over. It turned out okay.

She went on to summarize the key events in her memory:

Yeah, we had a lot of good times. It was fun. I remember our commencement primarily and moving up day. Also class day and ring day ceremonies. It was a big nothing, but it just [made] you feel and me feel good.[20]

D'Youville in the 1950s was growing, moving into nursing and healthcare. The staff took its mission of Catholic education seriously, as did the students. This tradition created serious attempts at integration as well as lingering participation in cold war anti-communism. It also continued its traditions of a vibrant, intelligent, but fun-loving, female student body.

ARIAL VIEW OF THE COLLEGE in 1959. The old buildings with the new dorm and Holy Angels are in the foreground. The new library is not very visible. The college is surrounded by houses on the other side of Porter Avenue and separating it from the Armory, behind is the huge abandoned laundry.

[1] *Statistical History of the United States*. Stanford, CT: Fairfield, 1960. Jill Ker Conway, "Faith, Knowledge, Gender." In Tracy Schier and Cynthia Russett, ed., *Catholic Women's Colleges in America*. Baltimore: Johns Hopkins University Press, 2002.

[2] Sister Mary Sheila Driscoll. *Heritage Series*. "D'Youville in the 1950s."

[3] *D'Youvillian*, 1950 and 1959.

[4] Janice Cooke Feigenbaum. "History of the Division of Nursing," pp. 7, 9-10, 12. *D'Youvillian*, 1955. Middle States Report, 1952, p. 19.

[5] Sister Mary Sheila Driscoll, "D'Youville in the 50s." *D'Youvillian*, 1950-59.

[6] Middle States Report, 1952.

[7] Middle States Report, 1952, p. 29. *D'Youvillian*, 1950, 1959. Progress Report to Middle States, October 1, 1959. Evaluation Middle States 1953-1979, Box I. D'Youville Archives. Middle States Reply, Op cit. Susan Carter, "Academic Women Revisited." *Journal of Social History*, 14 (Summer 1981), 675-99.

[8] *D'Youvillian*, 1950, 51, 53, 55, 56, 57, 58, 59. Interview with Joseph Grande.

[9] Report of the Inspectors of D'Youville College, February 26, 1953.

[10] Interview with Sylvia Grandesa.

[11] *D'Youville Magazine*, 39:4 (June 1950), p. 3; 44:1 (November 1954), p. 5; 47:4 (December 1948); 48.1 (March 1958).

[12] *D'Youville Magazine*, 39:3 (November 1950); 40:3 (November 1951); 45:4 (December 1954); 49:1 (March 1959); 46:2 (June 1956); and passim.

[13] Interview with Sister Mary O'Connell. Interview with Joseph Grande.

[14] *D'Youville Magazine*, 40:3 (November 1951); 42:3 (November 1953); 44:3 (November 1956); 48:1 (March 1958); 48:2 (June 1958); 49:1 (March 1959) and passim.

[15] *D'Youville Magazine*, 45:3 (November 1955); 46:2 (June 1956); 48:4 (December 1958).

[16] *D'Youville Magazine*, 43:1 (January 1953) and 44:3 (November 1954). *D'Youvillian*, passim the 1950 and particularly 1958 and 1959.

[17] Interview with Sister Rita Margraff.

[18] *D'Youvillian*, 1955, 1956, 1957, 1953. Grande interview.

[19] Interview with Grendesa.

[20] Interviews with Margraff and Koscinski.

Chapter Six

"Times They Were A-Changing" – 1960s

When Sister Francis Xavier became the twelfth president of D'Youville College in 1962, she presided over a college that was bounding in growth and change. Enrollment grew from 688 (with 494 in arts and sciences and 194 in nursing) to 1,250 (with 694 in arts and science and 556 in nursing). By 1967, D'Youville stood high in the ranks of Catholic higher education institutions – 36% had fewer than one hundred students and only 6% had more than two thousand students. The number of students was growing all over the country given both the war and post-war baby booms: five million extra students enrolled in college courses in the 1960s.[1] The additional students at D'Youville required more teachers, more accommodations, and more support services.

In 1961, twenty-four sisters and five priests taught at D'Youville. They were joined by thirty-three lay faculty (eleven men and twenty-two women). This roughly half and half division between lay and religious faculty reflected the past (as does a 3 to 1 ratio of female to male instructors). By 1969, the faculty had grown to 115, a 54% increase, and while the number of religious faculty fell slightly to twenty sisters and five priests, the number of lay faculty increased from thirty-three to eighty-five. The gender ratio also dropped from roughly 75% female to only 56%. In 1961, the twenty-four sisters of the faculty were the best educated with eight holding some form of the doctorate and eleven having master's degrees. In contrast, the males on the faculty, including the priests, numbered sixteen with four doctorates, two licenses (above a master's), and four master's. By 1969, the sisters remained well educated. There were seven doctorates among the twenty sisters teaching, but the male faculty now numbered thirty-four (with five priests) and they held twelve doctorates and one license. The intellectual weight seemed to shift away from D'Youville's tradition of the sisters being the most highly educated among the faculty.[2]

102

In 1960, D'Youville administration seemed to be the president, an academic dean, a dean of nursing, treasurer, a registrar, and a librarian – all Grey Nuns. By 1965, these positions remained, although a layperson, Virginia Ego, was dean of the School of Nursing. In addition, five laypersons served as directors of Adult Education, Development, Admissions, Health Service, and Information Services. The director of Admissions had a lay admissions officer and Mrs. Anne Lum was the alumnae secretary. By 1969, the yearbook showed (besides the president) two sisters serving as deans, one as treasurer, and Sister Mary Kathleen Duggan as the vice president of Academic Affairs. Two laypersons served as vice presidents of Administration and Development,

Graduation in 1967 in Kleinhan's Hall. The graduates have traditional roses.

and Virginia Ego remained as dean of Nursing. These lay leaders were aided by administrative committees of twenty-six men and women (of which eight were sisters and five were men). Sister Francis Xavier instituted the changes in the faculty and the growth of administration. She may have

> "We had to wear stockings all of the time, EVEN IF WE WERE WEARING SLACKS we had to wear stockings and if we had socks on, WE HAD TO WEAR STOCKINGS."

realized what this meant for the future. Sister Denise Roche, who joined the order in the 1960s, was urged to do graduate work in sociology because Sister Francis Xavier knew that she would need a sociologist in a few years.[3]

If growth of the student body led to profound changes in the nature of the faculty and the growth of administration, the most visible change at the college was physical. By the late 1950s, a new library and Madonna Hall had been built. Two additional apartment houses were purchased as temporary residence halls. That was not enough. Construction of a new dormitory was announced in May of 1962. It would have nine floors with twelve double rooms, two single rooms, a proctor's suite, guest room, study hall, and snack bar on each floor. The college dedicated Mary Agnes Hall in October 1964. Even before that dedication, an additional $10 million development plan was presented to the public. The college planned another dormitory, a health science classroom building of five stories, a fine arts building, a student center with gymnasium, swimming pool, and a dining capacity for one thousand, a faculty residence (primarily for sisters), and a new chapel. The college accomplished about half this plan. In 1965, they broke ground for the Health Science Building, expanded to six floors. They dedicated it in 1967 and broke ground for Marguerite Hall, the dormitory, and the college center (the dining area was reduced to about five hundred). In 1966, residence space was leased temporarily from the Stuyvesant Hotel. The plan was ambitious. A new Fine Arts program became a reality in 1964 but its building was never started. Nor was the new residence for sisters. The new chapel never started.[4]

For students in the early 1960s, D'Youville remained a conservative institution. The dress code was rigid. "We had to wear stockings all of the time, even if we were wearing slacks we had to wear stockings and if we had socks on, we had to wear stockings."[5] Another graduate of the 1960s remembered being the last class to wear academic gowns for the senior year. It "was not unheard of that we would wear white gloves and be invited to tea parties." A dropout from the period recalled, "I just didn't like it because it was too much like high school. I had to take French, I had to take Latin, I had to take Science . . . It seems I went from Catholic girls' school to a Catholic girls' school."[6]

The alumna who thought the dress code a bit rigid also recalled, less than fondly:

> Having to pick up your report card as a resident student . . . you obtained it from the president of the college and she was a . . . nun [with] traditions imbedded in formality, so what it involved was walking in to get the report card and backing out, because you weren't

103

In 1963 this group of six nurses went from graduation directly into the Navy as officers. An ROTC program with Canisius College allowed this transition.

allowed to turn your back to the individual in the office–the president of the college . . . It was always nerve racking getting your report card.[7]

The rules could also be quite strict.

I think as a group of women, we had a lot of fun; we would go out on Friday night and go to dances and have a good time. But I do think there was an intent to make us well behaved young women; that wasn't always successful. I remember Madonna Hall . . . one of the dormitory house mothers saw a young woman making out a bit too energetically in the yard of Madonna Hall, and, unfortunately the woman was expelled. So we were all in shock when that happened. The rules were very strict, and, in a way, inappropriate I think.[8]

The old warmth and intimacy of the college was remembered by the daughter of a faculty member who later attended the college.

Searching for cobwebbed nuns in the musty attic above the chapel in the main building, running in the annex where my dad's office was, near the statue of the shepardess Joan of Arc, running toward that fascinating elevator that led to the red tiled . . . basement library. I remember the soothing voice of Mrs. Gredel and Mme Ki Barland, the French teacher . . .[9]

Fine teaching continued as a tradition of the college. Interviews commented on many individuals. One was Ruth Seitz.

In 1968 parents enjoy a sing-along at Parent's Weekend. Capping was a highlight of these festivities.

She taught a methods class for education, and I utilized her . . . [in] my future classroom situations . . . She used to have very large classes and she managed it really well . . . We learned how to teach math or how to teach English.

Another commented:

Miss Ruth Seitz [was] the finest educator I have ever known . . . [She] was knowledgeable, professional, approachable, patient, and very disciplined. To this day, I think of her when I need to show my students patience. [She had] remarkable wit, I remember her answer to the question, what would she like to come back as in the next life—she said, 'a red-haired slide trombone player.'[10]

106

Another well remembered teacher was Father Donald Beechler. One traditional student said, "He was quite unusual in terms of his views of Catholicism and . . . shocked me in terms of his views." Another remembered more fondly:

Father Beechler, just because he was so dynamic; he taught us theology and he was very provocative and intellectual. . . . he introduced us to contemporary philosophy. He really forced us to think about things so that we no longer were just little girls from the local high school; we had to think on our own and we appreciated that.

Ruth Kelly remembered Beechler as "just fantastic, and really made me think. [He] kept on saying theology was different from religion . . . I like theology a lot." She also described a small trick the students played on Father Beechler:

After I left D'Youville, I got married and I had children, but my friends stayed here and I kept in touch with them. Father Beechler always said he would not give you back your term paper . . . unless you named your first child Donald . . . So my friends were visiting me and asked if they could borrow my son, who was only six months old. It was Halloween, so we brought him to school and none of the students went into the classroom, we just put my poor son in a nip and nap . . . on the desk and on the blackboard they wrote 'my name is Donald. I want my mother's term paper.'[11]

D'Youville continued its tradition of a strong religious orientation. Moriarty recalled the sheer joy of the tradition, "The college was very much Roman Catholic heritage college and I really always went to Mass here, [I] love this Chapel here, got married in this chapel, so I found it very helpful to me, that spiritual strength." Ruth Kelly recalled a more active sense of Catholicism, one combined slightly with the college's support of civil rights:

> I was active in something called . . . the Legion of Mary . . . We used to meet and . . . hear about people that needed someone to meet them and pray with them . . . We would get addresses and we would go visit people to see how they were doing . . . I remember that one of the people I was partnered with was an African American girl . . . I grew up in the suburbs. I didn't know any African American people, and she and I would go visit . . . people in nursing homes. . . . The African American people would be very glad to see a young African American girl.

The student newspaper expressed shock when D'Youville delegates attending a meeting of the National Foundation of Catholic College Students found that no Masses had been scheduled.[12]

Other traditional concerns continued among the students. Throughout the decade the Moving Up Day festival included the floats of each class and a parade. Until the late 1960s, the traditional yearbook dance, sophomore dance, residents' dance, sorority dance, and junior prom were formal affairs at fancy off-campus sites. In the late 1960s, these events seemed to be relegated to more general parents, sophomore, and junior weekends. Some student activities expanded. The girls' basketball team by 1964 played a six game schedule, splitting victories with Rosary Hill, beating Saint Bonaventure twice, and winning from Niagara University and Nazareth College.[13]

Although alumnae indicated disgust with the dress code, a contemporary article defended the ban on sneakers at the college. Students ran campaigns in both 1964 and 1967 to get a D'Youville student recognized in the *Glamour* magazine "Best Dressed on Campus" contest. The first blue jeans to appear in the *D'Youvillian* were worn by a mother during parents' weekend.[14]

Despite D'Youville's traditions and the generally protected and Catholic young ladies the college attracted, the changes of the 1960s toward equality and greater self-expression and participation had to affect the college. The growing student body was

A formal picture of the cheerleading squad in 1965. There may have been more cheerleaders than members of the basketball team.

107

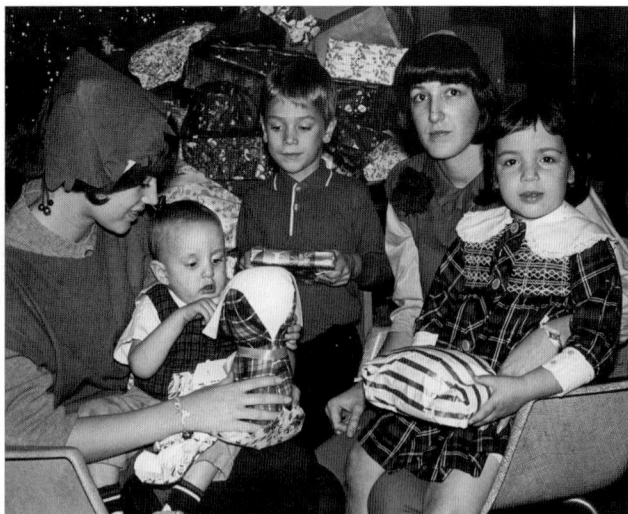

Two students from Sodality, Judy Koleznski and M. Kathleen Denecke, entertain children at the Christmas party in 1966.

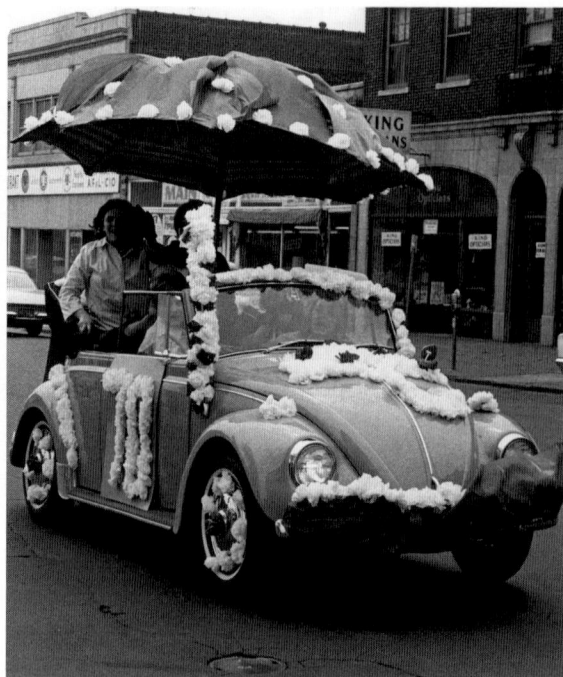

MUD could also be less formal. The Volkswagen above is decked out for the parade, but with a certain humorous flair.

108

more diverse. In 1960, 83% of the graduates came from Buffalo or western New York, with over half coming from the city itself. By 1969, only 35% came from the city and over a third came from outside the local area or beyond New York State. Students came from a variety of areas, including New York City and its suburbs, and brought a variety of experience to the college.[15] Some of the change they responded to was supported by the Catholic Church or its affiliates, for example, civil rights. In May 1960, *The Disc* ran an article somewhat critical of the sit-ins as a method but supporting a petition drive to further challenge Woolworth's department stores. (The faculty strongly supported this position.) John F. Kennedy was the choice in a campus poll in November of 1960. In 1961, articles in *The Disc* attacked the John Birch Society (which was founded in western New York) and applauded the rejection of a campus chapter of the conservative, Young Americans for Freedom (both the Young Democrats and the Young Republicans achieved recognition on campus, but the Young Democrats had a more consistent presence). In 1962, a note appeared urging the reading of *Ramparts*, a Catholic journal which evolved in the '60s to a noted radical magazine.[16]

Long-term activities kept D'Youville students in contact with the larger academic world. D'Youville students were champion debaters, winning at the regional level and being invited to debate at Harvard University. Students continued their participation in Model United Nations meetings and helped staff such a United Nations for high school students. National Student Association representatives not only brought demands about civil rights back to the campus, but also demands for Student Academic Freedom. Professors, also concerned in this area, organized a chapter of the American Association of University Professors.[17]

Student institutions at D'Youville changed in response to the new interests. The old *Mary's Mantle* put out as part of Sodality, became the general student newspaper – *The Disc*. *The Disc* was

The tradition of a court and queen for MUD continued in 1967. Note the long dresses and hats reflecting the past.

awarded Medalist rank by the Columbia Scholastic Press. (The name changed during the decade to *Patchwork*, *Sigillum*, and *Compendium*.) Student government expanded and altered itself (to take in more areas of concern). Its curriculum committee continued and actively criticized courses. After five decades, the student support for the *D'Youville Magazine* ended and it stopped publication in 1964. Even before its collapse, the journal had changed. Twice as many poems appeared (later a poetry magazine would be formed). The review featured far fewer pieces on Catholic culture with sociological and literary materials being reviewed. The journal also reviewed William Carlos Williams, Salinger, and *The Last Hurrah*, calling it a true Irish American classic. A review of D. H. Lawrence's *Lady Chatterley's Lover* condemned the book on the grounds that Lawrence claimed that only sex made us human. Ayn Rand's amoral views of power were also condemned. Both *To Kill a Mockingbird* and *Lilies of the Field* were cheered.[18]

As indicated earlier, President Kennedy was popular with these students. The magazine ran an editorial in April of 1963 condemning conformity. After his assassination, an editorial appeared lauding his call to sacrifice. Student memory of the assassination was vivid:

Sister Francis Xavier speaking at the ground breaking of the new Health Science Building in 1965. HSB remains one of the principle classroom buildings. It was later renamed Alt, after a distinguished alumna, Pauline Alt.

> We were in Mr. Grande's class and we heard all this noise in the hallway and I believe we were freshmen and we didn't know what was going on. And the noise got louder and louder and girls were sobbing and crying and Mr. Grande hated to be interrupted—he hated any distraction—so someone went out to find out what was going on and it turned out that the president had been shot—President Kennedy. And it was really unbelievably sad for us, the whole school was just in mourning.

The Kennedy appeal would remain strong. In 1964, Eunice Shriver visited the college to bolster the feelers of her brother Robert Kennedy for a presidential run.[19]

The real world intruded into students' lives, particularly those in the nursing program. A nursing student, Patricia Ryan Dudek, described three different nursing rotations:

> We had to work 3-11 pm at Our Lady of Victory Hospital. We were in charge. I remember one night when I was told that I would be getting a burn patient from Bethlehem Steel. I was real nervous about how I was going to handle it. But, their first aid was so good. They had dressings on it and everything. So, it worked out okay.

Students in the new biology lab in HSB (Alt) in 1967—dissecting a frog.

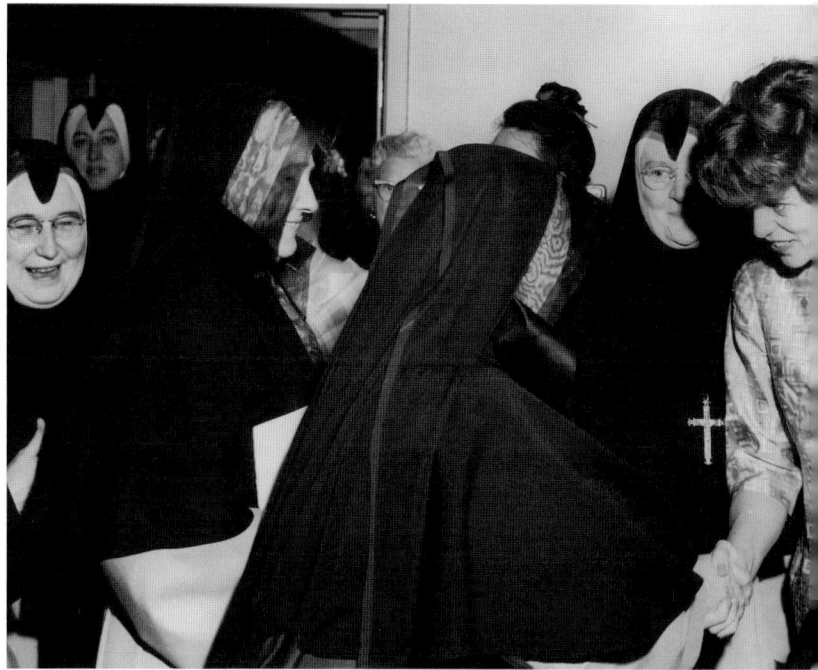

In 1966 the college honored Eunice Shriver (President Kennedy's sister) with an honorary degree. She greeted the Grey Nuns of the college.

At a rotation at Linwood-Bryant (psychological) Hospital, she commented:

> We didn't wear uniforms there. One of the nurses kept trying to give me meds. I guess she thought I was one of the patients.

Working:

> On a locked ward at Meyer Memorial I took care of a woman who killed her kids, and another one who had drowned kids in Delaware Lake. I remember feeling very sorry for them . . . I learned that people don't fit into the slots we make for them. It made me re-evaluate how I see people.[20]

Alumnae rarely reported sexual activity in the Oral History Surveys, but some risqué behavior was noted:

> We used to have these spring outings—and after one of these spring outings, the president of the college had been called and told that one of the girls on the bus had mooned someone in the car following. And she was fit to be tied. So she went in and got the whole class gathered together in the theatre hall and said 'this is really a disgrace to the college and I want the girl, the young woman, who did this to stand up.' And the entire class stood up.

A class in the 1930s had also stood up as one but not protesting this sort of behavior. As the incident reported earlier and the one above indicates, D'Youville students were probably part of the sexual revolution of the late '60s, but one has little idea as to the extent.[21]

111

One of the new buildings of the 1960s was **Mary Agnes Dormitory**, named for Sister Mary Agnes, the first dean of students. Notice both the *Peanuts* and the Kennedy stickers. Mary Agnes was later sold to be used as an adult-care residence. The college's ADOPT-A-GRANDPARENT PROGRAM would function there.

Another view of the biology labs in HSB (Alt) in 1967 with the anatomy of a cat in question.

By 1965, Vietnam became the center of student protest. *Patchwork* carried letters debating the policy in 1965. By 1969, students demanded to take part in the broad strategy put forth by the Students for a Democratic Society – Mobilization I. The new president let the faculty handle this and a quiet sit-in (rather a study-in) was held in the Blue Lounge. Later, faculty would accompany students to broader demonstrations. Alumnae asked about this remembered few details – administrators saw a deeper sense of protest.[22]

Not all students rejected the war. One nursing graduate, Eleanor Alexander, volunteered in the Army Nurse Corp. In 1967, she died in a plane crash in the mountains of Qui Nhon – one of eight women, all nurses, who died in the war. Professor Antanas Musteikis also spoke in favor of the war as necessary to prevent the spread of communism. Sister Denise Roche, who was a young colleague of Professor Musteikis, wondered at this. Many of the most rebellious students were sociology majors (the field in which they both taught), but he never seemed to have trouble with them.[23]

Lecture hall in HSB (Alt) in 1968.

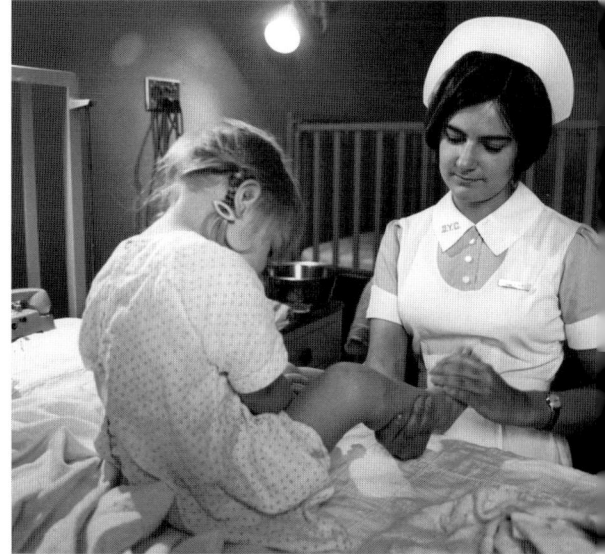

Education also extended beyond the campus. A D'Youville student nurse responds to a child in the hospital in 1968.

One alumna of the period, Marcella Farinelli Fierro, 1962, wrote, "Dr. Antanas Musteikis taught the best soc class ever." Musteikis, Beechler, Grande, and to large extent, Ms. Ruth Sietz, and many of the teaching sisters fit a pattern–later referred to as the "old lions"–properly dressed (or in habit) demanding respect and attention, devoted to their subject i.e. presenting an adult role. A young faculty member (with a

115

Zella Caple, who taught dance at the college for twenty years, leads a class in the 1960s.

radical student background) from a few years later remembered arguing over lunch but always with courtesy and a sense of academic equality. That clearly was how a conservative scholar kept his young charges in line.[24]

While student rebellion seemed to have been limited it may have played a role in creating tensions in the faculty. By 1968 these tensions along with illness caused Sister Francis Xavier to resign. (She later founded the Grey Nun Office of Development and served in many advisory positions in nursing education.)[25]

In 1968, when Sister Mary Charlotte assumed the presidency, she faced a crisis that could have overwhelmed anyone. As early as 1960, D'Youville's Board of Governors, who met yearly to approve

A D'Youville student teacher does storytime for a group of children in 1968.

diplomas (its sole official function), had informal discussions about state interference with Catholic colleges. A few years later they expressed concern about growth of Catholic junior colleges and advocated a Board of Catholic Higher Education. These warnings seemed questionable as D'Youville continued to grow. In 1964, the Board of Governors was abolished with the agreement of Middle States.[26]

Even with growth, the college was not stable. The treasurer's report from 1962-63 showed fees met only 77% of educational costs; the remainder came from the contributed services of Grey Nuns. Resident fees did cover the interest and debt for Madonna Hall. By 1967-68, fees covered only 73% of education costs and even after a Grey Nuns donation of $279,000, there was a $100,000 deficit. To meet cost, the new dorm would have to have a 75% occupancy. The combined interest on the various constructions would add another $378,000 to that deficit. More tuition might have covered costs, but freshmen enrollment in nursing peaked in 1965 and in liberal arts it peaked in 1966. By the late '60s, both Niagara University and Saint Bonaventure had become co-ed. D'Youville girls were actively hanging out in the Canisius library.[27]

116

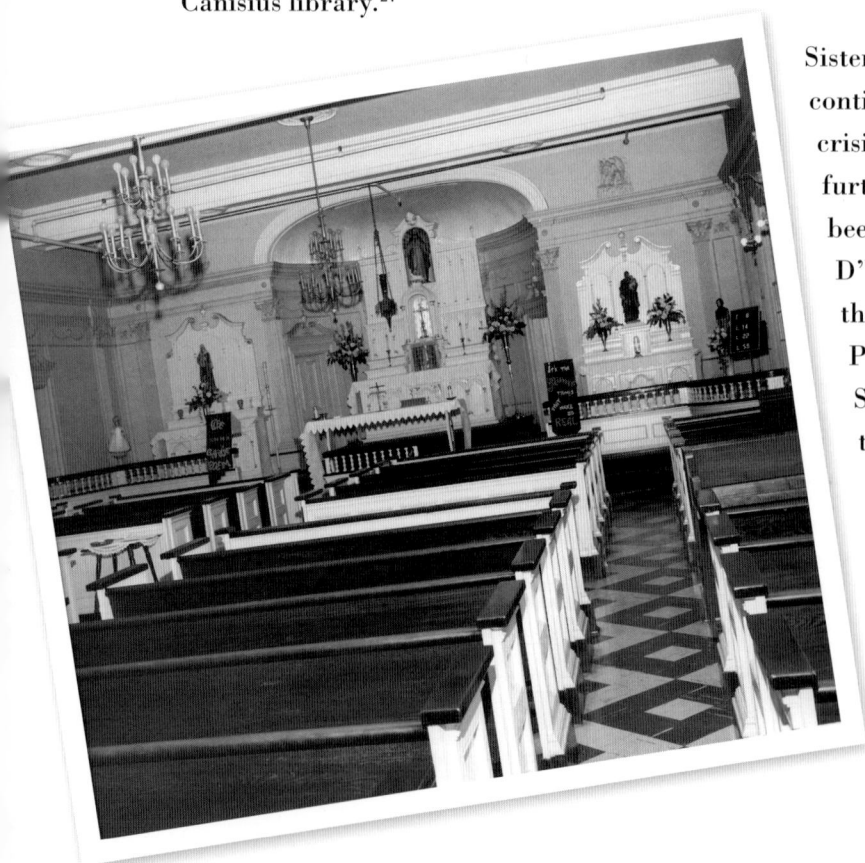

Sister Mary Charlotte came in to face the continued student rebellion; a growing financial crisis, an enrollment crisis, co-education, and further questions in the 1970s. Times had been a-changing, perhaps not the best for D'Youville. But of the alumnae quoted here, three went on to master's degrees, three to PhDs, and one to an MD. The most critical, Suzanne Lavin, got an Irish scholarship that changed her life. She went back for a master's degree in Irish studies, met a young man from Colorado, joined him there as a teacher, lived for a while on a

The D'Youville chapel remained a place of peace and contemplation for the campus in 1967, but notice the removal of a portion of the communion rail that recognized changes in Church practice.

commune, helped organize protests in 2006 on immigrant exclusion, and in the end, had this to say, "I was influenced by seeing women in positions of authority . . . I think that I never was afraid to show leadership, or use my talents, because I saw women doing that."[28]

[1] Sister Mary Sheila Driscoll, *Chronicle of D'Youville College. Sigillum*, March 3,1967 (campus newspaper). Thomas Bonner. "The Unintended Revolution," *Change*, 18 (September-October 1986), p. 44-52.

[2] *D'Youvillian*, 1961, 1969.

[3] *D'Youvillian*, 1960, 1965, 1969. Interview with Sister Denise Roche.

[4] Sister Mary Sheila Driscoll, "D'Youville Chronicle." *The Disc*, October 5, 1962; December 17, 1962; May 2, 1963; October 6, 1964; *Patchwork*, May 10, 1965; *Sigillum*, February 2, 1967; April 30, 1969.

[5] Interview with Judith Schiffert.

[6] Interview with Suzanne Lavin. Interview with Ruth Kelly.

[7] Interview with Judith Schiffert.

[8] Interview with Suzanne Lavin.

[9] Typescript only, from Dante Musteikis-Rankis, D'Youville Oral History Project.

[10] Interview with Mary Ellen Moriarity. Typescript Danute Musteikis-Rarkis.

[11] Interview with Dr. Karen Piotrowski. Interview with Suzanne Lavin. Interview with Ruth Kelly.

[12] Interview with Mary Ellen Moriarty. Interview with Ruth Kelly. *The Disc*, October 4, 1963; *Sigillum*, March 17, 1967.

[13] *D'Youvillian*, 1960-1969, particularly 1964, p. 206 and 1968, p. 70.

[14] *The Disc*, November 9, 1962, February 2, 1964; *Sigillum*, March 17, 1967. *D'Youvillian*, 1968.

[15] *D'Youvillian*, 1960, 1969.

[16] *The Disc*, May 12, 1960; November 3, 1960; May 12, 1961; December 14, 1961; November 9, 1962; *D'Youvillian*, 1960-69.

[17] *The Disc*, May 12, 1960; December 14, 1960; April 7, 1960; April 5, 1962; May 3, 1962; December 17, 1962; October 10, 1968. *The Disc*, May 12, 1960; December 14, 1960; April 7, 1960; April 5, 1962; May 3, 1962; December 17, 1962; October 10, 1968.

[18] *The Disc*, February 15, 1963. Sister Mary Sheila Driscoll, *Heritage Series*, the '60s. *D'Youville Magazine*, 1960-64, particularly June 1960, November 1960, December 1961, June 1962, November 1962.

[19] *D'Youville Magazine*, 52 (April 1963); 53 (December 1963). Interview with Suzanne Lavin. *The Disc*, October 3, 1964.

[20] Feiganbaum. "History of the Division of Nursing," p. 15-16.

[21] Interview with Suzanne Lavin.

[22] *Patchwork*, December 10, 1965, February 11, 1966. *Compendium*, March 26, 1969, October 8, 1969, November 6, 1969. Interview with Mary Ellen Moriarty. Interview with Karen Piotrowski. Interview with Sister Mary O'Connell. Interview with Sister Mary Charlotte.

[23] Feigenbaum. "History of the Division of Nursing," p. 17. *Compendium*, December 17, 1969. Interview with Sister Denise Roche.

[24] *D'Mensions* (Winter 2006), p. 24. Thomas Benton, "Remembering the Old Lions," *Chronicle of Higher Education* (April 2, 2004), p. 2-3.

[25] Interview with Sister Rita Margraff. *D'Mensions* (Spring 2005), p. 24.

[26] Meeting of the Board of Governors Book, 1960, 1962, D'Youville College Archives. Report of Evaluating Committee, Middle States Association of Colleges and Secondary Schools, 1964. Evaluation Box 1, D'Youville Archives.

[27] Report of the Treasurers 1962-63, 1967-68. Administrative Fee 1961-1972. D'Youville College Archives; Annual Report 1969-70 Admission, Ibid. *The Disc*, October 4, 1963, November 8, 1963.

[28] Interview with Suzanne Lavin.

117

Chapter Seven

The College Changes – 1970s

Sister R. Patricia Smith (formerly Sister Peter Damian) congratulates a graduating senior as dean of Liberal Arts in 1973. Note she is in academic robes not a habit. Sister R. Patricia would later serve in the library, as director of building and grounds, and eventually return as a colleague in history. Her work is cited earlier.

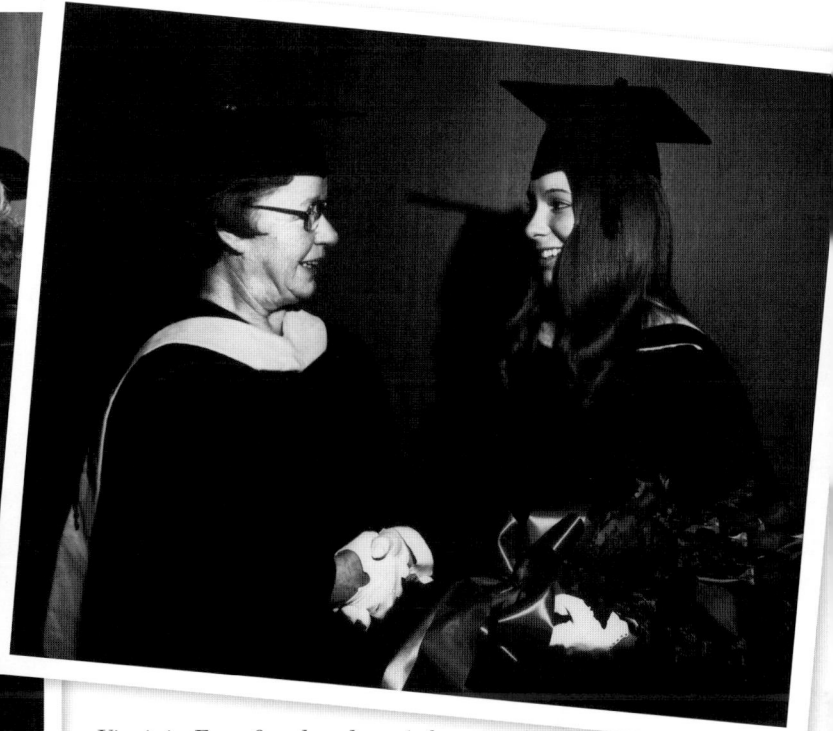

Virginia Ego, first lay dean (of nursing), congratulates a graduating senior in 1973. Note the traditional bouquet of roses.

The financial crunch at D'Youville by the end of the 1960s might have been unique, but a whole series of problems struck Catholic colleges for women at this time. Catholic men's colleges began to admit women. The liberal arts declined even at Harvard University. Each Catholic woman's college attempted to find some particular appeal – competency-based education at Alverno College in Milwaukee, education of African American minorities at Saint Xavier in New Orleans. President Norbert Hruby of Aquinas College in Grand Rapids stressed the urban location of these colleges, advocating bringing the humanities to the broader scene. Some saw the growing need for technical education as a solution to the problem. The concept of the urban university combined both Hruby's notion, the technical, and looked to a new kind of student. "Students were characteristically older, attended part-time, scored lower on entrance tests, were employed, and tended to come from lower socio-economic backgrounds."[1]

When Sister Mary Charlotte Barton arrived to be the thirteenth college president in 1968 (with a broken foot) she would face all the problems of the 1960s and the need to transform the college. She came from the difficult position of having to close the D'Youville Academy in Atlanta because it faced the possibility of becoming a middle class means to marginalize integration (the academy had been integrated earlier in a modest fashion). Sister Mary Charlotte presided over movement to a lay board of trustees and the move to co-education. She faced changes in the expectations of women created by the rise of feminism (and the last throes of the student movement). She also faced a changing

119

The class of 1975 prepares to march at Klienhans. There are four males in the procession and only one young lady is wearing the formerly required white gloves. ———————

Sister Mary Charlotte Barton, president of the college, Dennis Pines (an early male graduate), and Eileen Hanley lead the baccalaureate procession in 1979. Sister Mary Charlotte served during some of the most trying times at the college. ———————

sense of the Catholic Church in the Vatican II announcements and the impact they had on both lay Catholics and the sisterhoods.[2]

Sister Mary Charlotte helped organize a lay board as part of her initial reform. Four sisters still sat on the Board but the majority was lay and it met in Buffalo. (The old Board was all sisters and met at the mother house in Yardley, Pennsylvania.) Sister Mary Charlotte was fortunate that she acted first in this area because a crisis was brewing in enrollment. The number of nursing majors entering in 1968 dropped by almost half (the nursing class of 1971 graduated 146; that of 1972 a mere 79). Enrollment in education was also falling. By 1971, the college failed to pay its clerical staff – it was virtually out of money. The building of the 1960s left considerable indebtedness. Sister Mary Charlotte, with the help of new Board members, drew up a business plan, won interviews with bankers, and eventually a loan to allow the college to survive. By 1973 the college leased out Mary Agnes for use as a nursing home. In 1976, the lease was converted to a sale. The lease paid for finance changes, the sale eliminated a good portion of the debt.[3]

The move to a lay broadening and changing the mission of the college to be in the Catholic tradition also allowed D'Youville students to access state loans and state Bundy grants and national aid to both nursing and to students in general. Sister Mary O'Connell was brought in to run financial aid.

> I opened my little envelope and it said you are assigned to D'Youville College . . . Sr. Kathleen Duggan was acting president at the time and I called her up and said Kathleen what am I going to do at the college and she said what do you think? I said put cherries in the salads in the dining room and she said how did you know?

120

Sister Mary was so good at the job she was hired as a consultant by the federal government, and she loved it. "We did have a lot of money at the time which was wonderful for the students, so I got a chance to help a lot of students . . . I think the Democrats were in and we were . . . getting money."[4]

Even though funding became available, the college also focused on recruitment. The administration made students aware that they should help sell the college. Sister Mary Charlotte also announced tuition increases and a drive to create an annual giving campaign. The student newspapers interviewed the new head of the Board of Trustees, Edward Kavinoky, who stressed he was there to develop funds for survival. When the diocesan teacher's program ended, the students were again asked to help recruit. In 1972, an Office of Institutional Advancement came into being under Robert Beechler with the charge of raising $1.5 million. As late as 1978, a Student Service, Skill, Time Committee was pictured painting one of the college buildings. Early in the crisis, the college expanded the recruitment staff so that five full-time recruiters worked throughout the decade.[5]

In 1970, in part to deal with enrollment, the new Board announced that men would be allowed in D'Youville. The idea of men at D'Youville was quite strange. A few years before when they planned the new college center, Professor Grande noticed an omission. "There was no men's locker room! I said you know, D'Youville's not ready for a shared locker room, I'm quite

And the building goes on. Sister Francis Xavier in 1968 with the architect of the college center, Don Maharon (the one who didn't include a men's locker room).

Ellen Smith, library director (second from right in the first row) and the library staff including the Audio-visual staff of Ken Hintermeyer and Irene Walsh (middle). Several in this picture are still part of the library staff or employed elsewhere by the college.

Sister Virginia Carley from the 1974 yearbook. She was deeply beloved by the students and faculty. She spoke with a soft drawl and was nicknamed Dixie. ———————————

122

Sister Denise Roche as a young faculty member in 1969. Similar photos exist for the early 1970s, but this shows her in the modified habit of the Grey Nuns before they decided to adopt everyday dress. ————————

sure . . . I mean, they have guests coming for anything, they gotta have a men's locker room! So that's how we got it." When the question came up among the sisters, Sister Mary Charlotte reflected:

> We had a history of women's education and yet I felt if we were a women's college and that was our tradition and we knew how to do that, we probably would not have a disproportionate number of male students that would radically change the fabric of our background.

The major concern noted by Sister Mary Charlotte as well, were questions of leadership. Sister Rosalie Bertell had objected:

> I thought they should remain a girls' college and form a Catholic University of Western New York and have a girls' college in the University, but you know, not everyone would play . . . My experience was the girls took leadership positions. The minute they started taking boys, I think they were up for president of student government, the girls were stepping back and letting the boys do all the leadership, so I didn't like it, I didn't think it was good.[6]

The student newspaper introduced students to the idea and conducted a broad survey – few thought it would change the college and only nineteen said they would leave over the issue. Sister Rosalie was wrong about leadership – the yearbooks of the 1970s show no male class officers or student government officers in the first two years, never more than two in any year until 1979 and then only two in the Senate, one in Residence Council, and one in the Programming Committee. Indeed, the initial male entrants received psychological and emotional support. Paul Gospodarski remembered, "Father Bill Smith would meet us each morning, and pull out a deck of cards. If he pulled out an ace, we went to class. Anything else, we skipped the day." He also recalled that some situations were less than ideal for the male ego.

I was holding a baby in the newborn nursery and the baby did its thing – all over my new, clean, pressed, white uniform . . . the baby kept crying. Mrs. Kemp [the clinical instructor]

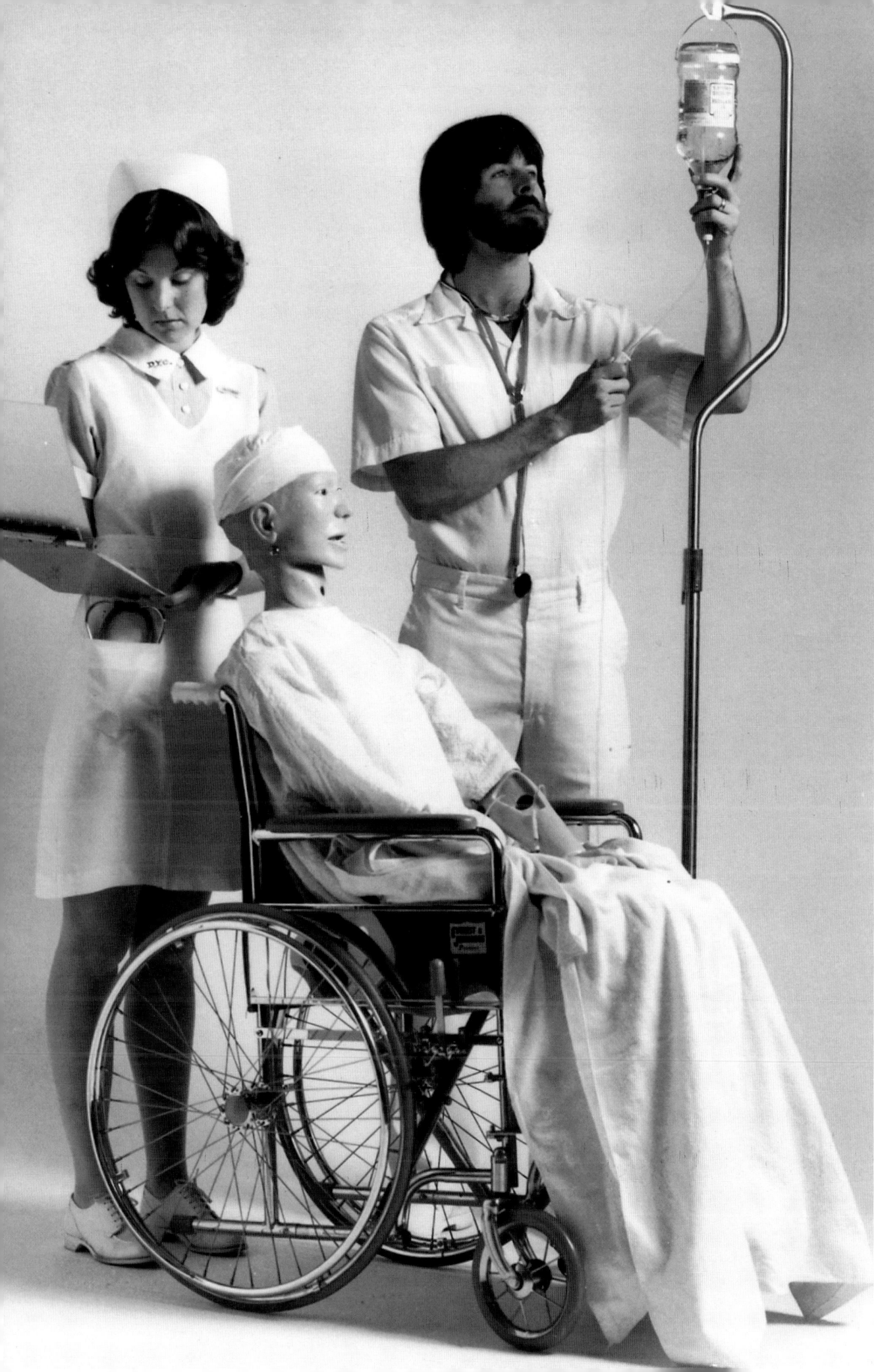

told me to rub the baby's head and he'll stop crying. That worked, but I wonder if that [experience] is why I never wanted to take care of babies after that.[7]

While nursing enrollment recovered in the 1970s, indeed by 1976, of 1,419 full- and part-time students, 1,107 were in the Division of Nursing. Included were part-time students, usually older women returning to school after rearing children. D'Youville sought these women by the creation of an active continuing education program. Part-time enrollment grew from 228 in 1970 to over 400 in 1978 and equaled 167 full-time students. Some of these returning students needed extra help and qualifications of other entering students may have eroded slightly. To meet these needs (and allow D'Youville to recruit students who had become marginal to the system of higher education) the college created a Learning Center in 1976. For a time, the college sponsored a Center for Women in Management. Sister Mary O'Connell remembered recruiting.

> In one bank I was in, the girls came for workshops, the secretaries, and I told them if you're not happy in your job, you know, change it, find something else. Don't go on in your life not being happy with what you're doing. And the president's secretary quit at this bank and he wasn't very happy with me.

As Sister Mary Charlotte noted, these new students were:

> Very refreshing, I think for some of the faculty too, to have people that had been out there and were taking things more seriously than someone coming in as a freshman . . . I think that getting older students was a wonderful mix.[8]

124

One problem that arose with the entrance of male students was dormitory space. Eventually space became available for men in Mary Agnes dormitory and that forced a more open policy on dorm visitation, etc. These changes also led to more open policies on alcohol use. New York State law allowed eighteen-year-olds the right to consume alcohol. In 1971, a new policy allowed alcohol at college functions and in 1977, alcohol was allowed in the residences for those over eighteen – the dean had to approve other uses. These student demands reflected the continued radical thrust from the 1960s that still played a role on the campus.[9]

Sister Mary Charlotte also faced continued student radicalism. The environmental movement began and students celebrated Earth Day on campus in 1970. The Vietnam War continued and students continued to protest. Both Vietnam and racial demonstrations led to student riots about police presence on the campus at the University of Buffalo in the spring of 1970. In the midst of these heady days, D'Youville students wanted to join the demonstrations in downtown Buffalo. They did it with the accompaniment of several faculty members. *Compendium* contained articles on the Irish question supporting the Catholic position in Northern Ireland, reprinting material from the Vietnam moratorium committees, supporting the Massachusetts law declaring the war unconstitutional, demanding the right of eighteen-year-olds to vote, and even a pro-abortion article. The *Compendium* issue in April of 1971 was a virtual peace issue. When George McGovern lost the run for presidency in 1972, the *Compendium* response was that he was too honest.[10]

Later in the 1970s, the carnival moved into the gym but the clowns remained popular.

The college responded with understanding, sympathy, and tradition. A whole series of speakers were allowed (or sponsored on campus). The first was Mrs. Malcolm X in the spring of 1970. The next spring saw the Catholic anti-war radicals, the Berrigans, on campus. *Compendium* later reported their trials. In 1972, Ralph Abernathy spoke at the campus on the continuing civil rights struggle. In October of 1973, Congresswoman Shirley Chisolm spoke. (While not a radical, she did represent the achievement of both civil rights advocacy and feminist agitation.) In 1974, Cesar Chavez, leader of the militant farm workers, appeared on campus.

The vibrant and beloved Sister Virginia Carley wrote challenges on some issues for *Compendium*. In April of 1970, she rather directly attacked the pro-abortion article that had appeared. At other times, she was more subtle, suggesting for example, that Christ was the only way to true peace (in the midst of the anti-Vietnam controversies). She also commented on feminism, below.[11]

The radical issue to which there was a variety of response at the college was feminism. The issue arrived slowly – there was real pride when a D'Youville student became Fire Prevention Queen in October 1970 and each year a student competed in the *Glamour* magazine contest for best dressed. But as early as 1970, *Compendium* included an article showing that a mere 1% of college women chose the career of homemaker/wife in a recent survey. In the same issue, Sister Virginia commented that love drives us, not careers. When *Roe v. Wade* was decided by the Supreme Court in 1973, *Compendium* did not support the decision but did suggest prevention was better than abortion (prevention was not quite in Catholic doctrine either). When the feminist movement hit full stride, *Compendium* published pieces on consciousness raising. One alumna characterized her group as "baby boomer brats, burning bras, and marching in parades and kind of putting religion to one side." By 1975, the cherished tradition of capping nurses drew critics among the faculty. One faculty member called the cap a symbol of servitude. A student recalled a more gentle reason for dropping the ceremony:

> One of the reasons we stopped the capping is we added male students. The male students felt left out of the capping. They actually got white painter's caps and wanted to have the white painter's caps put on which was kind of funny.[12]

The feminist agitation, unlike most radical issues, continued into the later 1970s. Representative Chisolm's visit to the college in 1973 was a spark to issues. The same issue of the *Catalyst* also questioned equity in women's sports. In 1978 Professor Fay Friedman brought a symposium of Buffalo's women in political office to campus to a large audience. By the late 1970s, the *Catalyst* ran an article demanding Catholic ordination of women.[13]

As the *Catalyst* article mentioned, life in the Catholic Church was shifting. These were the years of Vatican II which opened Catholicism to the world. The life of the sisters changed. Sister Rosalie Bertell, who was teaching math at the college, wanted to leave after suffering a heart attack. But she was convinced to stay because Middle States was coming. She agreed but only if she lived off campus. Since the sisters were paid $100 per month, this wasn't possible unless she took a job at Roswell Cancer Institute and Kevin Cahill, an English professor, brought her to and from her residence with the Sisters of Saint Joseph. (Sister Rosalie went on to found the International Institute of Concern for Public Health

126

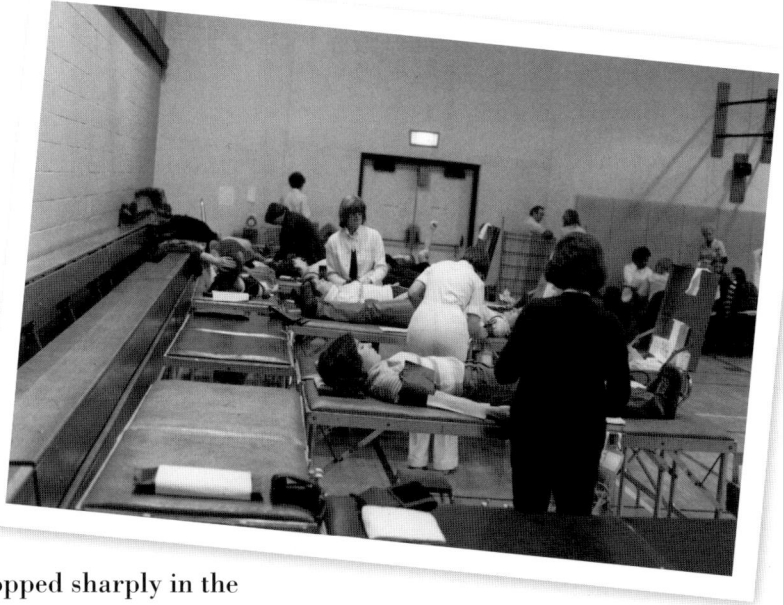

From World War II, blood collections were common at the college. In the 1970s these drives became major campaigns.

in Toronto.) The independence of the sisters was one reason for their gradual transition to work beyond the college. Sister Mary Charlotte Barton raised the pay of the sisters (most of the funds went to the order) so that the budget would allow lay faculty to replace them. The number of young women entering the orders dropped sharply in the 1970s. In 1972, fifteen sisters (of differing orders) graduated from D'Youville; that was never repeated. The sisters also dressed without their distinctive habits. As reported by Sister Rita:

> We had to buy patterns and squeeze the pattern onto whatever amount of material we had in our habit. So Sisters James Francis and I, we did a lot of sewing but we had to use what we had. We weren't buying material as yet, and then we did thrift shopping . . . we used to wear cloaks, big black cloaks. We even made coats out of those.

127

Sister Mary Charlotte recalled using the leadership of Father Theodore Hesberg of Notre Dame to understand the changes. Certainly the sisters' lives changed but so did the religious life at the college. The rise of an ecumenical spirit was evident as the college became more diverse. A student article commented, "There is more religion around than ever . . . Those involved in anything ecumenical soon realize that brushing up against various religious traditions must sharpen one's religious stance."[14]

Social life at the college did not change because men were present. As indicated earlier, they did not assume the leadership positions and only reached 10% of the student body by the end of the decade. The growth of the number of older students and to some degree minority students did alter the social feel at the college. Through the decade, traditional student activities declined. The MUD Carnival, mixers, and semi-formal dances still were celebrated. In the fall, the students put on Parents Weekend with the capping ceremony (which grew controversial). Other weekends disappeared. Student area clubs declined. D'Youville chorus, capable of putting on a concert at the start of the decade, dwindled to fifteen members. Formal dances were replaced by coffeehouse or other professional entertainment. The Halloween party became a honky tonk night. Mixers and TGIFs prevailed but in 1973 a *Catalyst* article complained there was only one mixer and the lack of social life was a reason to leave the college.[15]

Like other traditional activities, sports also suffered. Sports had never been a major emphasis at the college, but in the early 1970s, teams played against larger schools like SUNY Brockport, Geneseo, and

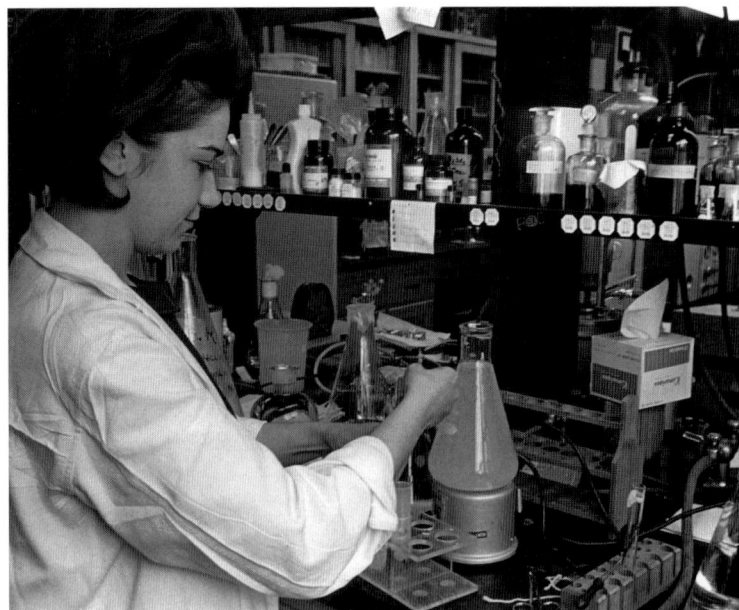

Chemistry needed to be worked on in 1977 just as it had in earlier decades. The equipment does seem newer. ———————

128

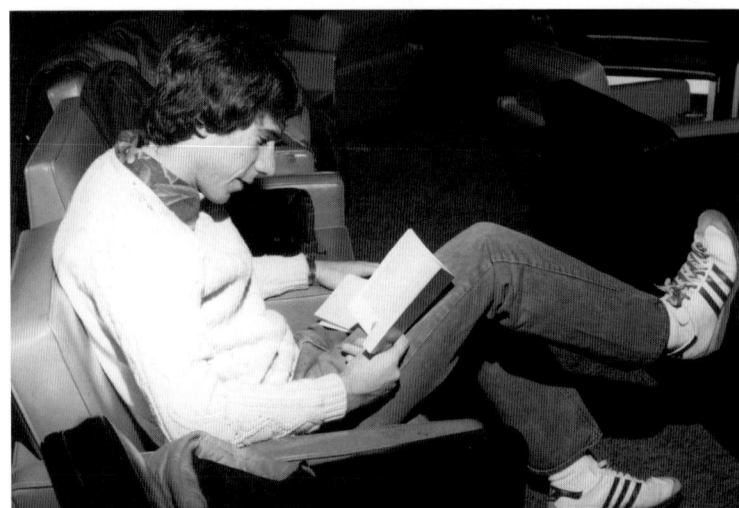

In 1975 students used the Blue Lounge for study space. That custom died out and this picture would be rare today. ——————

Binghamton. D'Youville girls swam against the University of Buffalo in 1970 and beat them in a volleyball game in 1972. A girl's doubles team in tennis got to the Northeast Regional Tournament in 1971. The first men's team was in basketball in 1972 with seven players. Throughout the decade the team usually had seven to ten members. The women's basketball team usually had eleven to thirteen (enough to scrimmage). Despite hiring a sports director in 1978, the decline was apparent. In 1979, it looked as if the tennis team would not draw enough players to compete. The director did move toward general fitness rather than competition. In 1979, the school bought its first weight machine. That year they attempted to organize a jogging club.[16]

Some aspects of college social life responded to changes in recruitment. The slow increase of African American students coupled with civil rights activism led to a Black Student Union (BSU) on campus. The BSU grew from fifteen in 1974 to twenty at the end of the decade. From the beginning they organized to raise money for a scholarship to aid one of their members – part of the tradition of the college for the Spring Honors Convention. Usually the funds were raised through sponsorship of a gospel choir concert which brought an element of African American culture to the campus as well. An attempt to accommodate the greater numbers of commuter students and older students came in the creation of Free Activity Time (FAT) in the middle of the day in 1976. In 1979, the college modified the Wednesday schedule on a permanent basis to make FAT friendlier to students and faculty. Campus Ministry put on Saint Patrick, Saint Joseph, and later other ethnic tables both to raise money and have events open to wider participation.[17]

For many students, the college social life was not critical. A group of graduates from 1980 all said they came for study and academic training. The worst experience for one "[was] giving [her] first injection to a patient who was sixty pounds and it was an intramuscular injection and there [was] no muscle, hitting a bone and coming back out – an awful feeling for me." They described studying:

> We all studied together. We'd sit in the hallway opposite each other, Indian style, and just quiz each other . . . We never went out if there was a test. We would wait. We would take the test and then we would go out . . .

> We loved Elmwood, the Locker Room. It was predominantly a girls school. I think we had one floor of boys. We'd see guys from Canisius College on dates. The cops were our friends. They used to give us rides home because they didn't want us to walk from Allentown. We would go up and ask, or they would just offer — 'You girls are not going to walk through the streets alone.'

One semi-prank resulted from these fun nights out. These twelfth floor residents had been asked to carry down a Christmas tree.

> I didn't throw it, I opened the window. We asked or persuaded some freshman children to push the tree out the window . . . . We just threw it out the window. Thank God no one was hurt.[18]

As these stories indicate, drinking was part of the D'Youville social culture by the late 1970s.

In 1977, Buffalo was struck by a huge blizzard – since giving the city its snow reputation. A male student described the event.

129

> Since it was Friday, many of us were planning to go to Allentown and party at Birdie's 19th Hole and Mulligan's Brick Bar. When we tried to go over to the Student Center for lunch, we figured it was going to take us a little longer to get there and back. Marguerite Hall [the dorm] was maybe 100 feet from the entrance to the Student Center; you could not see the building.

The women's basketball team in 1978 with Coach Sheila Sloan. The squad numbers eleven and that size was usual through most of the team's history.

In 1978 the college, after years of rather LIMITED FINANCES, did manage to buy the OLD INDUSTRIAL LAUNDRY behind the campus. As SISTER MARY CHARLOTTE BARTON commented recently the only thing she got built was a parking lot (on the site of this building).

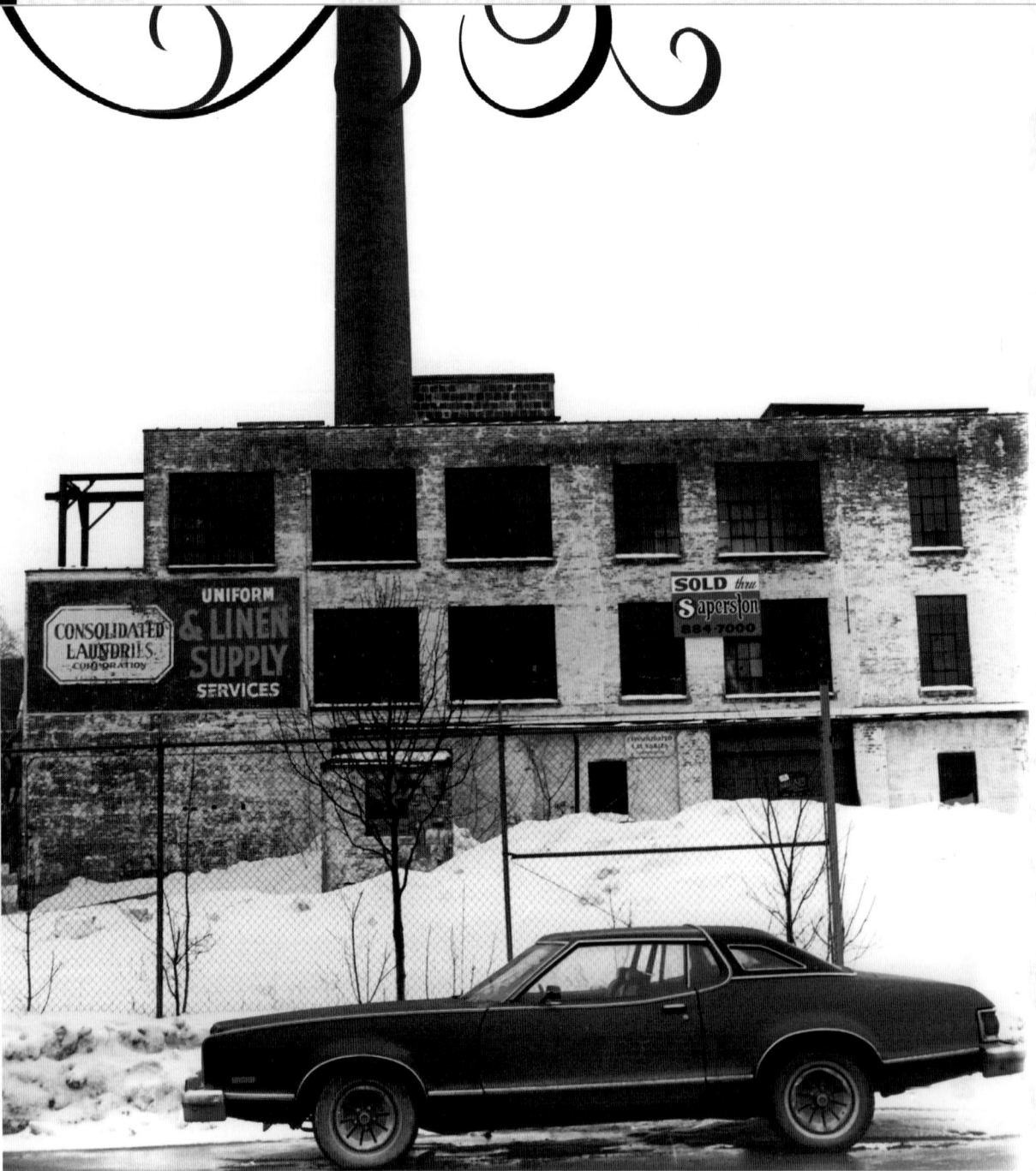

CONSOLIDATED LAUNDRIES CORPORATION

UNIFORM & LINEN SUPPLY SERVICES

SOLD thru Saperston 884-7000

At about 3 p.m. the TV news was saying that the entire area was shut down and a state of emergency was being declared. It was right at this time that it was announced to students stranded at D'Youville College that beer was going to be served that evening in the college center. I always thought that some officials at the college felt that some students would try to make it to Allentown and freeze to death.

> While the **COLLEGE CHANGED,** there remained a core of ideas that **SUSTAINED THE PAST.** The whole college community debated the curriculum and retained a set of courses **DEEPLY IMBUED** with the liberal arts.

Students did volunteer at the Connecticut Street Armory which was an emergency center and others helped check up on older folk in the neighborhood. Returning to Marguerite during the storm, Mr. Jurkiewicz saw a figure clinging tightly to a small tree just off the sidewalk.

> I turned around and went toward the shape holding on to the tree and heard a girl's voice say 'thank you.' I put an arm around her and brought her to the doorway and led her inside where she turned around and through her ski mask blew me a kiss and ran upstairs to her room. To this day I have never known who she was or what ever happened to her.[19]

The storm also caused several student protests, one was serious. When the administration suggested extending the year to make up lost time, forty or fifty nursing students objected.

> We went down to see – to make an appointment to see the dean and he wouldn't see even a representative. So we said, okay, we'll wait. So you know the whole side wing down there in between the elevators and Wilson Farms? We sat there. Just sat there to wait to see the Dean. And I do recall the secretary coming saying she had to use the restroom, could she get through and some of our . . . gentlemen students . . . said 'no I'm sorry, you'll have to wait.' Within minutes they came and said 'the Dean will meet you at whatever time this afternoon.' So we left . . . we had a sit-in.[20]

While the college changed, there remained a core of ideas that sustained the past. The whole college community debated the curriculum and retained a set of courses deeply imbued with the liberal arts. While the students often were at D'Youville for nursing, other majors like French were dropped (fewer French teachers in demand); they appreciated the liberal arts. One reported:

> I really fell in love with my philosophy courses. I finished [then] stayed an extra year [to finish] my bachelor of arts major in philosophy, so those courses were terrific for me because they were so outside of science, there was actually opportunity to think, to discuss, it was kind of interesting to look at issues.

131

Similarly, the ladies of the class of 1980 recalled:

> We like the intimacy. The teachers, you never felt like you couldn't go up and ask a question after class . . . I think my favorite was also Mr. Cahill because he made you think outside the traditional box. He didn't teach English in a way that was black and white. In nursing, in all our other classes, everything was always right or wrong . . . Ironically, we were nursing students,—yet it was English. There was one assignment – you could pick any song from hard rock to disco – any song whatever, but we had to write about beyond the words and what it meant to us.[21]

The professors reflected this interest in teaching and in teaching these more varied students.

> I have found that the students are . . . have over time become more, have more ability to be open with professors, comfortable with professors. It's not as formal a relationship as it used to be. And this allows, I think, the students the confidence to ask questions, to challenge perspectives, to give their own perspective on things, but I think that's more exciting.

Another simply relished the whole atmosphere, "Just the stuff in the classes, sitting down and talking to people, watching people grow. Teaching is a real kick and this is a real teaching institution."[22]

The old simple campus atmosphere that could go back to the start was at the college. One alumnus recalled:

> I would work in the summer . . . One of my jobs was to clean the labs, the Chemistry lab on the second floor . . . I would get all the glassware ready and I would make the lab ready. I used to ride my bike all the way, and I lived out on Grant/Amherst area [2 and 1/2 miles away on the West side].[23]

The college had changed; the financial crunch was over. D'Youville ran a small capital campaign in the late 1970s to tear down the rusted industrial laundry behind the college for parking and to restore the charming theater in the 1908 extension. But money was still pinched. "Professor Nielson, Dr. Johnson, and a group of us over the years used to meet at 7 or 7:30 in the morning and sit in

132

In 1979 the old school auditorium was redesigned into a beautiful small theater, now the Kavinoky Theater. Sister Denise Roche, now the president of the college, consults with the designers.

the hallway because our offices were too cold. We brought in a fireplace screen and we would have our fireside chats." And the college faced choices about its future under the new president, Sister Denise Roche.[24]

[1] Fennette Seabury and Joe Davis. "The Metropolitan University: History, Mission, and Defining Characteristics." *New Directions for Student Services*, 79 (1978), p. 9. (They are quoting an earlier study). Norbert Hruby. "Future of the Small Catholic College." *Religious Education*, 73 (Fall 1978), p. 35-41. Keller and Keller. *Making Harvard Modern*, p. 408. Thomas Bonner, "The Unintended Revolution." *Change*, 18 (Sept.-Oct. 1986) p. 44-52. Perusal of *The Education Index* for the 1970s.

[2] Interview with Joseph Grande. Interview with Sister Mary Charlotte Barton.

[3] Interview with Sister Mary Charlotte Barton. Sister Mary Sheila Driscoll, "The 1970s." *Middle State Task Force Report*, 1973, p. 27-28. Evaluation File to 1974, D'Youville Archive.

[4] Sister Mary Sheila Driscoll, "The 1970s." Interview with Sister Mary O'Connell.

[5] *Compendium*, 3:4 (December 1, 1970) p. 5; 3:5 (February 12, 1971) p. 1 and 2; 4:3 (November 18, 1971) p. 1; 6:2 (November 6, 1972) p. 1. *Catalyst*, 7:1 (September 1978) p. 2. *Compendium*, 3:1 (October 20, 1970) p. 5.

[6] Interview with Joseph Grande. Interview with Sister Mary Charlotte Barton. Interview with Sister Rosalie Bertell.

[7] *Compendium*, 3:1 (October 2, 1970) p. 2, 6, 10. *D'Youvillian*, 1970-1979; Janice Feigenbaum. "History of the Division of Nursing" (1992), p. 18-19.

[8] Feigenbaum. "History of the Division of Nursing," p. 21. Sister Mary Sheila Driscoll, "The 1970s." "Report to Middle States 1981. Evaluation Middle States," D'Youville Archives. Interview Sister Mary O'Connell. Interview Sister Mary Charlotte Barton.

[9] *Compendium*, 3:1 (October 2, 1970), p. 2; 3:5 (February 2, 1971) p. 3; 3:7 (March 26, 1971) p. 3.

[10] *Compendium*, 2:5 (March 23, 1970) p. 6-7; 3:9 (May 7, 1971). Interview with Sister Mary Charlotte Barton. *Compendium*, 2:5 (March 23, 1970) p. 1. *UB Today* (Winter 2005) 14-21. *Compendium*, 2:4 (February 27, 1970) p. 1; 2:5 (March 23, 1970) p. 11; 2:6 (April 4, 1970) p. 1; 3:8 (April 19, 1971); 6:3 (December 12, 1972).

[11] *Compendium*, 2:5 (March 23, 1970) p. 3; 3:7 (March 26, 1971) p. 1; 3:8 (April 19, 1971) p. 2; 5:1 (December 14, 1972) p. 8. *Catalyst*, 1:2 (October 19, 1973) p. 1; 3:1 (October 1974) p. 1. *Compendium*, 2:6 (April 24, 1970) p. 4; 3:4 (December 1, 1970) p. 1; 3:3 (November 13, 1970) p. 7.

[12] *Compendium*, 3:1 (October 10, 1970) p. 1; 2:4 (February 25, 1970) p. 3; 3:1 (February 1972) p. 1; 7:1 (February 20, 1973) p. 3; 3:3 (November 13, 1970) p. 7-8; 7:1 (February 30, 1973) p. 1. *Catalyst*, 3:4 (May 1974) p. 4; 4:4 (December 10, 1975). Interview with Rosetta Rico. Interview with Karen Piotrowski.

[13] *Catalyst*, 1:2 (October 30, 1973) p. 1 and 3; 7:3 (November 1978); 9:3 (October 1979).

[14] Interviews with Sister Rosalie Bertell, Sister Rita Margraff, Sister Mary Charlotte Barton. *Catalyst*, 5:5 (April 1977) p. 2. *D'Youvillian*, 1970-1979, particularly 1972.

[15] *D'Youvillian*, 1970-1979. *Compendium*, 2:6 (April 24, 1970); 3:1 (October 2, 1970) p. 8. *Catalyst*, 1:2 (October 30, 1973) p. 4; 1:3 (November 15, 1973) p. 2; 5:4 (May 1977); 5:5 (April 1977); 6:4 (November 1977) p. 3; 6:7 (April 27, 1978).

[16] *Compendium*, 3:3 (November 19, 1970) p. 3; 3:4 (December 1, 1970) p. 3; 4:2 (October 18, 1971) p. 3; 6:3 (December 12, 1972) p. 7. *Catalyst*, 7:1 (September 1978) p. 4; 9:1 (September 1979) p. 6; 9:2 (October 1979) p. 6-7. *D'Youvillian*, 1970-1979.

[17] *D'Youvillian*, 1974, 1977, 1979. *Catalyst*, 7:3 (November 1978); 9:1 (September 28, 1974) p. 3.

[18] Interview with the class of 1980.

[19] Report of Edward Jurkiewicz. Filed with the D'Youville Oral History Project.

[20] Interview with Janet Ihlenfeld. *Compendium*, 6:7 (April 27, 1978). The schedule was revamped to meet student objections.

[21] *Compendium*, 2:4 (February 25, 1970) p. 1; 3:7 (March 26, 1971) p. 1. Interview with Sister Denise Roche. Interview with Susan Nielsen, op.cit. Interview with class of 1980.

[22] Interview with Joseph Fennell. Interview with David Kelly.

[23] Interview with Marcia Zinteck.

[24] Interview with Jamie DeWaters. *Catalyst*, 7:1 (September 1978) p. 1; 7:3 (November 1978) p. 1.

Chapter Eight

Directions and Cross Currents

By going co-ed in the 1970s and through careful husbandry, D'Youville had survived as a college. The college was growing at the end of the 1970s but that growth was almost entirely due to nursing. Nursing had failed the college before so the situation was precarious. Almost no women's colleges existed by 1992 (a mere 84 serving only 2.3% of all students), so the choice to go co-ed had been correct, but women's colleges also had problems in making the transition. D'Youville shared in these problems. In 1979, the college had 1,550 students, 65.6% of whom were nursing students. By 1983, the number was down to 1,270, with about 61% being in nursing. Only business as a major grew in terms of percentages. By 1987, total enrollment was down to 981, with only 151 students living in the dormitory. Two years later enrollment was back to 1,259 students with 241 in the dormitory.[1]

The last great year of nursing classes was 1985-86, with 503 full-time and 68 part-time undergraduate nursing students, and 7 full-time and 57 part-time graduate nursing students. By 1989-90, nursing knew only 167 full-time and 139 part-time students, with graduate programs growing to 54 full-time and 48 part-time students. The college had anticipated this shortfall. In the early 1980s, a broad scale plan was written by folks from across the college. They wanted to reduce the dependence on nursing by

The 1983 graduation class seated across the first rows of the Kleinhans Auditorium. Compare to earlier photos where the class is on the stage. The administration and faculty now occupy the stage. ———

136

building business, computer science, areas in education like special education and bilingual education. The plan actually dropped several majors — psychology (as needing too many resources) and criminal justice (as not really in the mission of the college). The plan was ready by March of 1982, but it did not seem adequate to some. In September of 1982, Gertrude Torres became the academic dean. She had already been the center of controversy as an outside advisor and consultant who forced the nursing department into a more theoretical direction. She had also created the graduate nursing program at the college which required hiring more doctoral prepared nurses on the faculty. Sister Denise came up with the idea of having occupational and physical therapy as majors at the college. Dr. Torres suggested they should be five-year master's programs. By 1989-90, physical therapy was the major with the most full-time students (186 and 4 part-time students).

A graduate in 1983 getting a big hug from her father.

Occupational therapy had the fourth highest total after business (102) and education (97) with 96 full-time and 8 part-time students. Nursing remained larger overall (given part-time students) but the wonder of these two majors was that high demand meant recruiting traditional as well as older students, and freshmen instead of transfers. The dormitory numbers went from 151 to 240 from 1987 to 1989.[2]

Occupational and physical therapy fit both the long-term history of the college–its identification with nursing and medical subspecialties (the medical technology program) and presented a focus for the future. Dietetics was planned by the end of the decade as was a nurse practitioner program, and in the 1990s a physician assistant program would come into being. The medical fields fit the mission of the college and the idea of service. They also appealed to students from non-college families and to older students. Both groups wanted education that had immediate career implications. Some faculty were not pleased with the health care orientation but recognized the need.

> I was here when that happened obviously, and I think they thought they needed to find a niche that would allow them to grow and expand. And I think it made sense for them to build on their reputation at the time. It was a little difficult because I am in business so the accent was constantly on health and not on other areas.

Another noted:

> There was a real resistance in the faculty to graduate programs, to OT, PT, five-year programs. We were going down the tubes, I could recognize that, see that, and I said okay, if it saves us it saves us, do it . . . And they never undercut their support for the history department or the

137

Graduate Vernetta Billups with her niece in 1981. Graduation in recent decades seems to have become less formal and more family oriented, perhaps due to older graduates.

English department so it mattered relatively little. My model is that we should have been the MIT of health care . . . MIT [has] really strong liberal arts programs.[3]

By the 1980s the effect of the post-war baby boom was over and the eighteen to twenty-two-year-old age cohort dropped sharply. Even in the 1970s the college moved toward recruitment of nontraditional students. The last year when more than half of D'Youville students were in that age category was 1985. By the end of the decade, almost 60% (57.4) were older than 22. By the mid-80s, recruitment of men and of other minorities reached peaks. African American students were 11.9% of students in 1985; other minorities were 5.9% of students. By the end of the decade, those percentages declined and D'Youville students were almost 86% white. Male graduates rose to 16% of total graduates in 1986, only to drop back to under 11% in 1989 (by that year more than 20% of applicants were male, probably due to the new physical therapy field). In 1984, only 11% of D'Youville graduates were from beyond western New York. That percentage also began to drop in the late 1980s. By 1989, only 68.1% were from the western New York area.[4]

How did the college adjust to these shifting types of students? Adjustment to older students continued trends from the 1970s as these students reached 40% in 1985 and a majority thereafter. In 1980, the *Catalyst* ran a description of a returning nursing student, age thirty-five, with family and work responsibilities. By 1980, family events, like a pool party with children, became part of the yearly schedule. The Student Government was reorganized with specific senators for continuing education students. In 1984, the adult learners created their own organization and some demanded an on-campus daycare center. After a committee studied the question, a survey demonstrated very limited demand for an on-campus center and the school offered to subsidize some care at neighborhood centers. Later in the decade, membership in a senior honor society became available. Generally, returning adults found they fit in at D'Youville. Ruth Kelly noted the:

Second time I came here I'm 45 or so, but I didn't hang around with people my age . . . My friends were all traditional students and we used to go out a lot ... I went to Boston with these students, the Model UN course, and they made me go to the delegate dance with them; they said that there might be some advisors there I could dance with. So I had a very active social life the second time around, when these kids were all the same age as my own children. And I was the

Kevin Cahill hooding a student in 1983. Students chose who would hood. Cahill is remembered fondly by all the students he taught. He served as a mentor to many faculty and was a friend to all. ——————

139

only one who had her own place, so they used to come over to my house and watch Monday night football, regularly, and they'd bring popcorn and things.

The faculty really enjoyed the older students:

I do really love the diversity of the students, that they all come from different backgrounds. I have huge admiration for these people that want to make better lives . . . the older students, the adult students that are coming back.

But it remained a challenge. Jeff Platt, who worked most closely with such students, commented:

Now you see adults standing in front of you with their two children watching mom or dad cry because something didn't go right. And it's so much more challenging to see someone your age crying about something than a 17-year-old crying about how she has no friends.[5]

In the 1980s, more African Americans entered college but not at the rate of increase of white students. The percentage gap actually grew although there was an increase in actual students. African American

students on white campuses often felt very uncomfortable. A study at Ohio State University saw African American students as feeling discriminated against with some demand for separate activity. The separate organization of African Americans at D'Youville began with the founding of the Black Student Union in the 1970s. In the 1980s, the union had from twelve to twenty members. Its major event – a gospel concert to raise money for a scholarship – was featured most years in the *D'Youvillian* and the scholarship itself was presented at the annual honors convocation. The Black Student Union was accepted by the administration and the students. The same was

African American graduate kissed by two aunts in 1983; by then the college was more diverse in terms of student origins.

Baccalaureate 1983

true for the Latin American Student Organization – LASO was also founded in the 1970s and had as many as twenty-eight students in the 1980s. In the late 1980s, Jesse Jackson appeared on campus to support the candidacy of Justice Trammel for mayor of the city. One African American student remembered his experience:

> I came from Brooklyn, NY, predominately an all black neighborhood. I went to a predominantly all white high school, South Shore High School where the races didn't mix at all, and actually, once or twice before I graduated there were several race riots. I came to D'Youville, again a predominantly white school, but there was more of a closeness, togetherness, you had people from all over the state coming to D'Youville College. A small microcosm in the dorms and on the campus. I can remember speaking to some of my fellow dorm mates who (now it would be odd to hear in New York state) had never met someone black – they didn't go to school with them – they only saw them on television . . . Ogdensburg, I never heard of it; Conestoga, I never heard of it (laughing). Skaneateles, never heard of those places, some of the towns of my fellow students.

141

To continue these good feelings, Campus Ministry ran a simulation of discrimination, in the late 1980s. (Some individuals were labeled and consciously shunned – then all discussed the experience.)[6]

For some of the students on campus, life really didn't change from the 1970s. Young women studied hard and then went drinking.

> During exam time, there was all this 'theft' from the PVR (dining hall); taking stuff back so that we'd be able to study. Being up all night in the study lounge with papers everywhere, all over the floor, finishing those last papers, not being the only one up at 3:00 in the morning.

And the drinking:

> We always went to the mixers. And after the mixers we would tear down the streamers and stuff, wrap them around ourselves, find rides from God knows who to get down to Mulligan's Brick Bar and at the time Mulligan's Brick Bar was not a place for college students to be at but all of D'Youville was there.

FATHER RONALD PACHANCE (RIGHT) and Robert Nielsen (left) hooding students in 1981. While Father Pachance left the college shortly after this photo, Robert Nielsen has been a student favorite for generations, known for his ability to startle and make one think in a fresh manner.

Sister Denise Roche at graduation in 1988. At her right is Herbert Mennen, chairperson of the Board of Trustees. At her left is Sister Rosalie Bertell, noted in these pages as a student and faculty member. When Sister Rosalie left D'Youville she went to do cancer research at Roswell Park Cancer Institute and then to establish the Institute of Concern for Public Health in Toronto where her work defined health hazards in using nuclear power. She has been named as one of the twentieth century's most prominent women scientists. —————

Money was not a question.

> We didn't have any money – we had to learn how to budget to get out to nurses night at the Locker Room. Roll our pennies up. We almost lived like a marriage. We shared our money to get to go. If you had money this week, you shared. If you didn't, someone else would.

Another student remembered that mixers "used to be packed with 500 people coming through at different times of the night."[7]

144

Actually drinking at D'Youville (while these quotes suggest excessiveness) was probably in the moderate range. A survey done at the college showed 81% drank (and 76% came from families that drank), but the usual intake was two to three drinks per setting. A minority had problems; sixty individuals reported some school problems, forty-five individuals did something they regretted, and fifty-six individuals had drunk enough so they couldn't remember what they had done (these individuals could be overlapping). A national survey showed a drop in student drinking over the 1980s from 89% to 80% over the decade. D'Youville started at the lower number. D'Youville's quantity and frequency numbers were also lower than the national survey (the national survey was done on college students at Daytona on spring break, but it is some indication).

Actually, the college was concerned about safety and control and tried to move the drinking into a more controlled space. In 1981, the state and the college worked on an alcohol abuse program that was mandated for all colleges. In 1981, the Board of Trustees agreed to open a pub on campus and the Student Government contributed $5,500 for renovation. The students wanted to call the pub the Maggie D (after the namesake of the college) but that was not allowed. Greg Campus worked in the pub:

> I bartended there, assistant manager. We had events. It even brought the commuter crowd. People from the afternoon who had stayed out here, from the academics building would go over to the Pub for lunch in the afternoon. That brought more of the school together for a period of time.

Another recalled, "They used to have a little pub, with a pool table and such. So that was kinda nice to go and sit back and have a beer or two." In 1985, the drinking age in New York State rose to twenty-one and while the pub struggled a few years the college was forced to close it. In 1986, the school issued a tough alcohol control policy. (The senior picnic required designated drivers, for example.) Student anti-drinking articles began to appear by 1985 and by the end of the decade students organized a SADD (Students Against Drunk Driving) chapter on campus.[8]

One group attracted traditional and dorm student support and worked toward including older students – Campus Ministry. Father Bob Perelli and Sister Barbara Quinn were a dynamic duo. Saturday night Mass grew from thirty-five to eighty-five, and students felt in charge. Nate Phillips recalled:

> I remember Father Bob at the Blue Lounge Mass. The Blue Lounge was the most incredible comfortable place to be on earth at the time. It was just relaxing at the time. You were receiving

A baccalaureate procession in 1981. Clearly visible from front to rear are the always dignified Dr. Antanas Musteikis (right) who kept control of classes and took conservative positions when the world seemed to be cracking in the 1960s and 1970s. Left is Sister Marie Christine in her doctoral robes from the Universidad de Salamanca. She taught Spanish for years and was nicknamed by the faculty as Madre. Smiling between them is Dr. Joseph Grande (often quoted here) who is a noted local historian and who rose to be a successful academic vice president. Clear behind Grande is Dr. Paul Johnson whose courses on medical ethics and death and dying have helped nurses and others deal with complex questions in their professional careers.

Father Bob's words of wisdom, his spiritual message and things. I think that touched my life the most, having the experience with him and Sister Barb . . . We basically started the choir to supplement Mass because I thought that singing was a big part of going to church. We had the choir, they funded a director . . . There were 13 to 22 of us [who] would sing every Sunday at Mass.

Another recalled:

> All my friends were Catholic and I was the lone Protestant in the group. In those days they used to have Mass in the Blue Lounge at 7 p.m. on a Saturday night, so everyone would go out

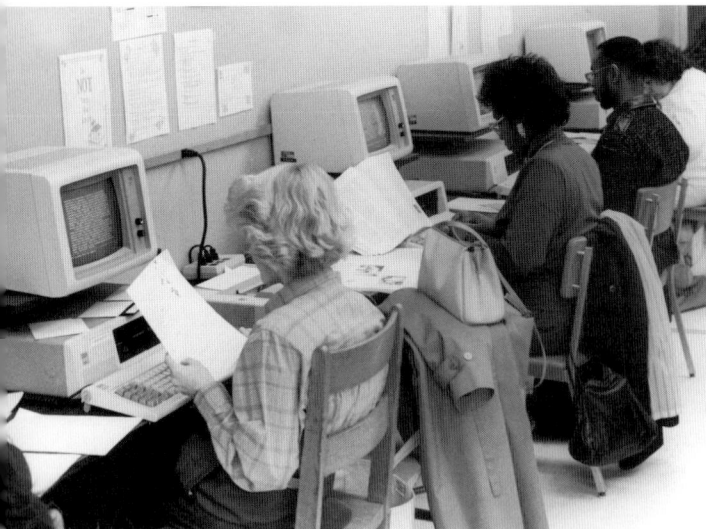

Students in the computer lab in 1988, time for final papers? ——————————

In 1989 an open-book final exam? ——————————

after. So they would say come on and I would say yes. That probably played a role in why I converted and became a Catholic. We all changed our clothes, because we had to be dressed up for Mass, then we all went to the park and played tag, played football, and other games in the snow.[9]

146   Campus Ministry reached out to older students by sponsoring ethnic tables. In 1982, there was a Polish feast and by 1984, a Spanish table and then other luncheon tables had been organized. Older students and faculty could contribute by bringing dishes. Campus Ministry used the funds generated to support various charities. Another broad perspective coming from Campus Ministry was a Peace Issues Campaign. In the Afghan Crisis of 1980, the Committee for Counseling Conscientious Objector literature was made available on campus. Campus Ministry sponsored activists William Sloan Coffin, Jr., and Dr. Helen Caldicott at baccalaureate services in 1983 and 1985. In the late 1980s, Campus Ministry put on extensive day-long or several days-long programs called Building Bridges which often had peace themes or themes to enhance interpersonal relationships (the discrimination game mentioned earlier).[10] Some of this was through charity, but they also helped at soup kitchens, etc. Part of this was the Adopt-a-Grandparent program at Mary Agnes (the home for the elderly that had once been a dorm). The ladies of 1983 got into the program when they attended a Campus Ministry meeting to avoid someone waiting to inspect their bags.

So we were given the adopt-a-grandparent program. Lo and behold, since we were not pillars of society, when we stood at free activity time to get people to join the adopt-a-grandparent, the program that [usually] had 10 or 12 people got 120 people and Mary Agnes Manor did not have enough grandparents to go around. We had to share grandparents . . . I do remember my Mrs. Rosenberg who was Jewish. I didn't know anyone Jewish in my life and she had lived all through Europe and she would tell me the most beautiful thing she had seen in her life was the sunrise over the Seine where she lived in Paris with her family. We painted together – I really didn't know much about painting but I had a little artistic bent about me.[11]

Other organizations formed and sponsored service activity. In 1982, Lambda Sigma emerged as a sophomore honor and service society. Its members served at college functions as ushers and monitors and ran independent projects as well. Throughout the 1980s, the Student Nursing Association organized semi-annual campus blood drives in cooperation with the Red Cross. In 1980, the campus saw the first CPR classes (which also continued thereafter). One of the big events through much of the 1980s was an annual dance marathon organized by the Student Council for Exceptional Children (SCEC). Young women committed themselves to dance continuously for up to twenty-four hours with friends paying money for each hour achieved. In 1980, $1,200 was raised for support of Children's Hospital. Later in the 1980s, SCEC began to volunteer for a skating with the handicapped program, which let young people with varying disabilities experience the joy of flashing about the ice.[12]

The two most dramatic acts of service of the 1980s were housing families of young people being treated at Roswell Cancer Institute and the rescue of Mary Agnes residents.

> Or even being [like a] family with the Roswell people living in the [lower level] of the dorm – a child, how everyone became responsible on campus about how Bethany was doing, how we participated and went through that as a family – we weren't the real family but we felt it. She had dinner with us all the time. How we felt when she was lost.

The second incident occurred during a rash of false fire alarms on campus. Some idiot pulled one at Mary Agnes, but students responded and helped residents evacuate the building in the middle of the night to the D'Youville gym (just across the parking lot). The students not only had to carry some residents down from upper floors, they also returned for bedding, clothing, and other necessities to keep the resident comfortable in the gym. Later, the students voted the favorite event of the decade was that Sister Denise bought pizza for everyone.[13]

Student life at the college continued to shift. Certain traditions like Moving Up Day continued with an expanded program to include older students, Bison baseball as well as the carnival, the mixer, and the one remaining formal

> The two most DRAMATIC ACTS OF SERVICE of the 1980s were housing families of young people being treated at ROSWELL CANCER INSTITUTE and the rescue of Mary Agnes residents.

dance. The two hundred days party and something at Halloween also continued. As did programs of outside talent brought into the pub, the gym, or the dining hall – such events could still draw more than one hundred students in the early 1980s. Senior week with its picnic continued, but the senior ball was gone after 1982 and the senior banquet after 1986. The alumni brunch and practice for graduation became highlights of the week.

Long-term traditions were ended. The most fought for was capping. In 1981, Gert Torres delivered an anti-capping speech at the capping ceremony. The next year it was cancelled. The Student Affairs (SA) funded a private capping ceremony that was controversial and then the practice finally ended.

147

Another tradition that died was an elaborate Christmas celebration called December Daze, which included a Wine and Cheese Party, a free lunch, and a mixer in 1982. It was replaced in 1987 with the more stately Presidential Christmas Party which was mainly for faculty and staff with some student leaders being invited.[14]

Sports also diminished. After 1983, there were no tennis or bowling teams. Men's basketball didn't compete in 1988 and 1989, and the only intercollegiate teams were women's volleyball and women's basketball. Student Affairs recognized these trends early and tried to organize intramural competition in the early 1980s, but this did not succeed. Even the ski club disappeared for a while. Aside from sports – the *Catalyst* itself failed to publish in 1987. By the late 1980s, new clubs like the Student Occupational Therapy Association and the Student Physical Therapy Association and new programs like the Competathon (starting in 1987) with its air band competition began to revive traditional student life.[15]

A survey done for Middle States in 1990 showed D'Youville students to be relatively uninterested in student programming; about half had gone to an intercollegiate athletic event. Two-thirds had been in the athletic facilities, more than 10% had gone to something sponsored by Campus Ministry or gone to a play at the professional theater (the Kavinoky) on campus. Three quarters had used food service and 80% had used the snack bar. D'Youville students seemed more like a national study of student patterns that fit the community college model rather than a more typical liberal arts college.[16]

148

One thing that both community college students and D'Youville students did was study, and the tradition of distinguished teaching continued at the college. The ladies of 1983 also remembered teachers that cared and challenged them.

Remember the time when we were in Mr. Cahill's class and he gave us those poems to analyze. Yours was "Puritan Adventures" to celebrate that you had just come to Boston with me and I got "Anthem for Doomed Youth." We had no idea what they meant and Sr. Carley told us she would help us. We had to meet in her office and she had to shut the door so that Mr. Cahill wouldn't hear her helping us put everything in the paper. Yours was about imagery and mine was this big complex thing about doom. Rosy – Thank you for letting me know. I looked mine up and no one in the

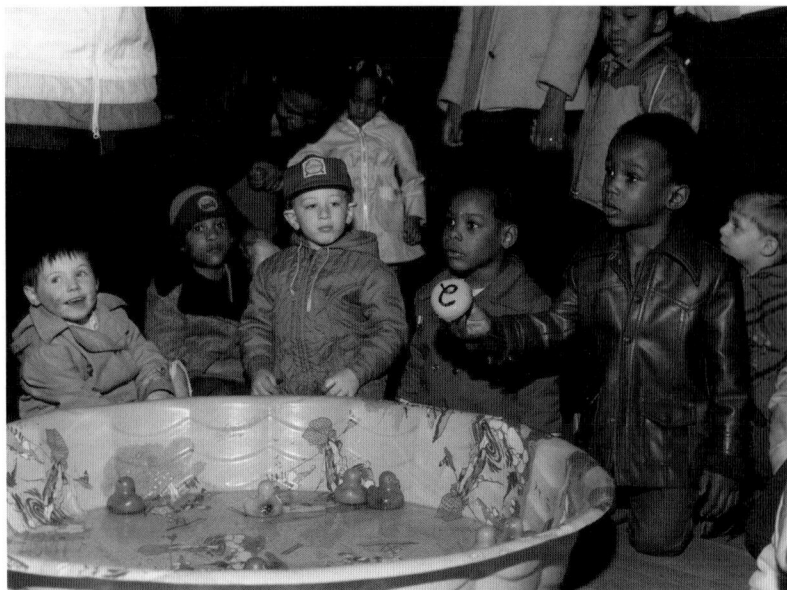

Some traditions remained in the 1980s. Children fish for a prize at the 1984 MUD carnival.

history of the world understood that poem. Cahill gave me this poem to figure out, I can't even remember the name of it now. I was so mad at him.

Sometimes the concern was more personal:

I buried my father, a sudden cardiac death and Patty and Gerry went around to all the professors and let them know what happened . . . Dr. Paul Johnson, Mr. Cahill, and Mr. Nielsen let me know they were there if I needed them . . . Let me know D'Youville really cared about me. I knew that very first nursing quiz that I took which was a couple of weeks later and I got a 'D' and I'd never gotten a D in my life. My nursing instructor hauled me into the room and said what happened to you and I told her what happened . . . She said maybe you should take some time off and I said I can't take some time off because my mother would kill me . . . She said 'you have to live in your head before you can live in her house' and I'll never forget the quote and it took some pressure off.

They remembered Mr. Nielsen's philosophy lesson:

He said you know you're going to be a nurse not 7 to 3, 3 to 11, you are a nurse 24 hours a day. You're on a bus, there's a [lost] child crying on that bus. That's your responsibility, that child is your problem because you are a nurse with every fiber of your being, he said. Emotionally, psychologically, you know, spiritually, socially. You take care of the child because you are a nurse. It's funny

Some traditions change. By the 1980s capping was gone. Dean of the college, Dr. Gertrude Torres, presents a nursing pin at the annual dinner. Dr. Torres helped introduce graduate work and both the physical therapy and occupational therapy programs at the college. ——————

In the 1980s dances still occurred, often in the pub; they were less formal and all were welcome to have fun. ——————

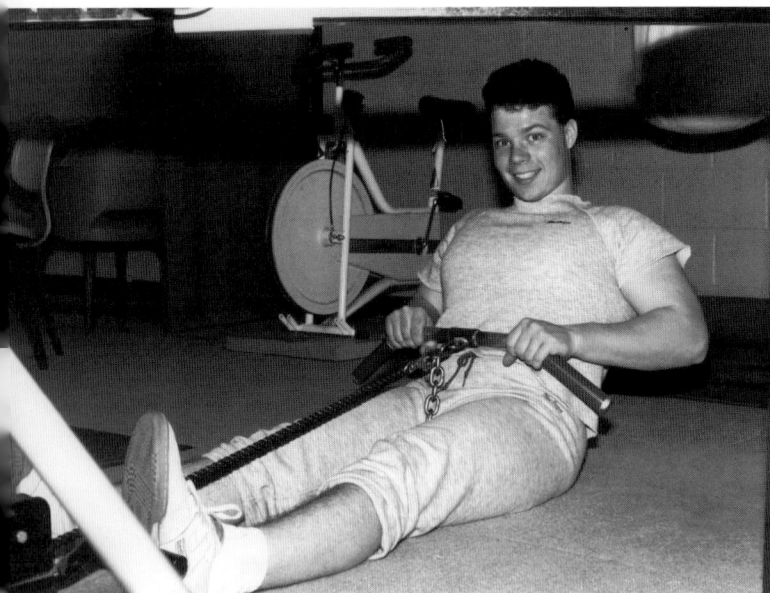

Some of the original equipment for the workout room from the 1980s. While the college still has this apparatus (it is off in the dance studio) the workout room has been vastly improved and is well used. It replaced the pub.

150

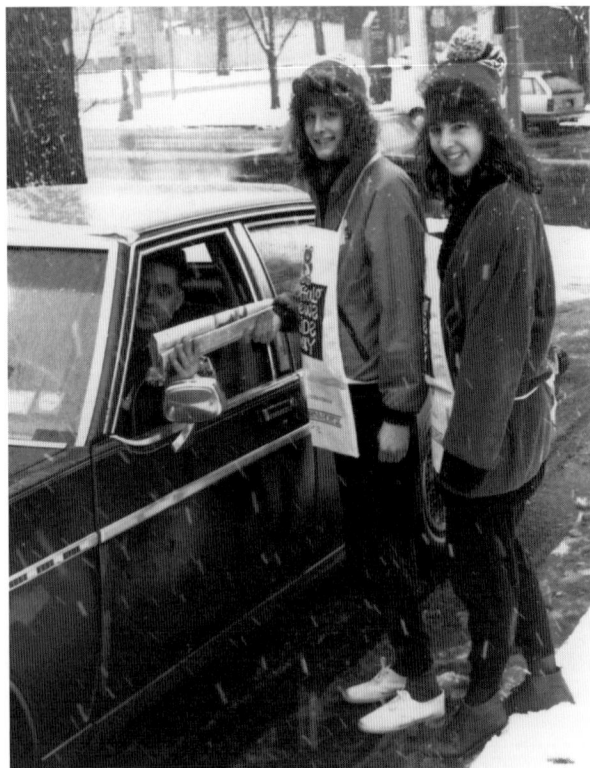

D'Youville students continued to work in the community. Two co-eds help with the Kids Day distribution to raise money for Buffalo's Women and Children's Hospital.

now we're in such political[ly] motivated work and political[ly] correct world and we were doing that 25 years ago. Where you didn't pass judgment and [you] learned culturally what this meant and how illness affected the family as a whole, not just the patient and how the wellness of the family and the empowerment of the family comes from the nurse.[17] Nathan Phillips recalled Dr. Jamie DeWaters from those years: She encouraged me to go above and beyond too. One of the things I [did] with her we did [as] an independent study [was] to do a conference on Special Education in areas . . . [where there] were weaknesses that should have been taught more, like how to do classroom management, how to set up your classroom and [how] to develop good rapport with students. We had people come in to speak about that, veteran teachers, we opened it up . . . to all the schools in Western New York and about 300 people attended.

About another teacher, Nathan, who is a large chap with great stage presence remembered fondly:

There was a Sister Joan . . . Sister Joan was very unique . . . She would always tell everyone to project your voice, project your voice (more loudly), until it came to me and she would tell me 'soften your voice you're gonna scare the kids...' Every time someone stood up she'd say 'now dear, remember to project your voice,' but when I stood up she would say 'bring it down.'[18]

After Sister Virginia Carley died of cancer in 1986, *Catalyst* ran the following in a banner,

"Maybe there is one last thing I can teach. Maybe I can teach people it's alright to die – everyone is so afraid of death, but it is like going home – its fine."[19]

The friendliness of D'Youville went from the top to the staff. Nathan Phillips again:

> I liked when Sr. Denise would just come and sit down at a table at lunch or dinner and really get to know the students. I felt like she was so approachable as president and that was mind boggling that she knew your name.

Further down the ranks, Irma Ramos, secretary in education, talked of the positive:

> The positive that I think [is] that D'Youville has an overall family orientation. I like the concern and care. The students, I can relate a lot to them – those students that are far from home, because I know what it is like to be away from home and have to get adjusted . . . They come in as freshmen and they're shy and then after a while you get to meet them and they're young adults. I have built up friendships with a couple of faculty members and I think that's nice, also with some students, like some of my mentees – I still keep in touch.

Mrs. Ramos originally came from New York City and found the college through a faculty member. The mentees she referred to were part of an ongoing program linking freshmen students to staff – a voluntary program on the part of staff. Other staff put it simply:

> The best thing about working for the college, the environment, nice people around. It's a nice place to be. Everybody here is like family, family oriented place to go. Less stress, no stress really. I mean because D'Youville to me has always been like a second family. You don't work someplace 18 years it it's not something special. It's pretty much how I look at D'Youville, it's an extended family. As far as the positive aspects, it has to be the people. The people are – the employees – the caring, the devotion, the loyalty. I've observed this for years, and it's what makes D'Youville. The people.[20]

D'Youville in the 1980s reached out to a wide variety of students – became more diverse in terms of ethnicity and minorities and in terms of age. By the end of the 1980s, new programs consolidated the orientation of the school and suggested a swing back to a more traditional student body. However, growth in the 1990s would have some of the cross currents found in the 1980s. No story is simple. Yet, despite trends in majors and varieties of students, the college remained devoted to good teaching and committed to an atmosphere of warmth and even love.

151

[1] John Thelan. *A History of American Higher Education*. Baltimore: John Hopkins University Press, 2004, p. 173. Andrea Hamilton. *A Vision for Girls, Gender Education and the Byrn Mawr School*. Baltimore: John Hopkins University Press, 2004, p. 346. Institutional Self Study, October 1984, p. 89-90, D'Youville Archives Evaluation Series Middle States, 1984-1992. Periodic Review D'Youville College, May 15, 1990, A4-A6, Ibid.

[2] Periodic Review D'Youville College, May 15, 1990, A4-A6, D'Youville College Archive. *Catalyst*, 11:10 (March 8, 1982); 12:1 (September 27, 1982). Feigenbaum, "History of the Division of Nursing", p. 23-24. Interview Sister Denise Roche.

[3] Interview with Joseph Fennell. Interview with David Kelly.

[4] George Kuh and Frank Ardailo, "Adult Learners and Traditional Age Freshmen," *Research in Education*, Vol. 6 (November 3, 1977) p. 207-219. Periodic Review D'Youville College, May 15, 1990, p. A4, A9, D'Youville Archives. *D'Youvillian*, 1984, 1986, 1989.

[5] *Catalyst*, (October 23, 1985); 9:8 (February 21, 1980); 9:10 (March 20, 1980); (November 28, 1984); (March 20, 1995). Interview with Ruth Kelly. Interview with Pat Palumbo. Interview with Jeffrey Plat.

[6] Therese Baker and William Velez. "Access to and Opportunity in Post Secondary Education in the United States." *Sociology of Education*, special issue (1996) p. 82-101. Mitchell Livingstone and Mac A. Stewart, "Minority Students on a White Campus." *NASPA Journal*, 24:3 (Winter 1987), p. 39-49. *D'Youvillian* 1980-1981. *Catalyst*, February 1986 and September 19, 1989. Interview with Gregory Campus.

[7] Interview with the class of 1983. Interview with Mary Pfeiffer.

[8] *Catalyst*, 10:5 (November 20, 1980); 9:9 (March 6, 1980); 11:3 (October 19, 1981); 11:5 (November 16, 1981), (November 13, 1985); (February 2, 1986); (May 7, 1986); (October 16, 1989). Interview with Gregory Campus. Interview with Marian Oliveri. Gonzalez, Gerado, and Elizabeth Broughton. "Changes in College Student Drinking and Alcohol Knowledge, A Decade of Progress 1981-1991." *Journal of College Student Development 34* (May 1993) p. 222-233.

[9] *Catalyst*, (March 1984); Interview with Nathan Phillips. Interview with Mary Pfeiffer. Interview with Jeanette Lesinski.

[10] *Catalyst*, 9:7 (February 7, 1980) p. 1; 12:10 (May 6, 1983); (May 5, 1985). 11:12 (April 5, 1982); (September 26, 1984); (October 6, 1985). *D'Youvillian*, 1983-1989.

[11] Interview with the class of 1983.

[12] *Catalyst*, 11:9 (February 22, 1982); (October 4, 1984); *D'Youvillian*, 1980, 1981, 1985; *Catalyst*, 10:2 (September 9, 1980); *Catalyst*, (November 14, 1989).

[13] Interview with the class of 1983. *Catalyst*, (November 14, 1989) and (December 15, 1989).

[14] *D'Youvillian*, 1980-1989; *Catalyst*, 11:5 (November 16, 1981) p. 1; 10:2 (September 9, 1980) p. 2; 10:8 (February 13, 1981) p. 1; 12:4 (November 22, 1982).

[15] *D'Youvillian*, 1980-1989. *Catalyst*, 9:8 (February 21, 1980) and 11:22 (April 5, 1982).

[16] Periodic Review Presented by D'Youville College, May 15, 1990. Evaluation File Middle States 1984-1992, D'Youville Archives. Leonard Baird, "The Undergraduate Experience: Commonalities and Differences Among Colleges." *Research in Higher Education* 31:3 (1990) p. 271-278.

[17] Interview with the class of 1983.

[18] Interview with Nathan Phillips.

[19] *Catalyst*, (February 12, 1986).

[20] In order: Interview with Nathan Phillips. Interview with Irma Ramos. Interview with Stephan Borowski (maintenance). Interview with Vince Ricchiazzi (maintenance). Interview with Tamie Watson (secretary, occupational therapy). Interview with Dr. Timothy Bronson (psychological counselor).

Chapter Nine

"The Nineties" – Growth and Diversity or Division?

From 1989-90 to 1999, the college grew from 1,259 students (full-time [FTE] equivalent of 1,032) to 2,152 students (full-time equivalent of 1,758). This 40+% growth in students (or 70% growth in FTE) was not simple or linear. The growth in the early 1990s was due to three programs – physical therapy, occupational therapy, and physician assistant. By 1995, these programs accounted for 696 students – counted as undergraduates (even though there was a fifth graduate year for two: occupational therapy and physical therapy) or 44.4% of all undergraduates. By the end of the '90s, the number had shrunk by fifty (physician assistant grew a bit) and the percentage had grown to 52.7% of total undergraduate enrollment. Other undergraduate areas shrunk more (nursing from 14% to 5% of the total). In 1999 there were only 1,234 undergraduates. In the late 1990s it was graduate enrollment that kept the overall college numbers up. Graduate enrollment both grew and changed. In 1995, the number of graduate students was 365 (with 47.5% of these in nursing fields – 173 students). By 1999 there were 918 graduate students: only 119 in nursing and 636 (69.3%) in some education field. Much of the graduate enrollment came from Canada by 1993-94. There were 323 foreign students, many from Canada. The subsequent enrollment in graduate education was heavily Canadian. The director of admissions would later claim to having the highest Canadian enrollment in the nation. D'Youville remained a lure for older students, even in the early 1990s. In 1989-90, only 42.5% were the traditional 18 to 22 year old students; by 1994 that slipped slightly to 37.19%. But looking at students from 18 to 29 years of age, the percentage in 1989-99 goes to 66.6% and remains there to the mid-90s – 68.3%. The early nineties had lots of fairly traditional students – the graduate emphasis of the later nineties would move age distribution a bit higher. The healthcare program may also have diversified the college. While minority groups as traditionally conceived (African American, Hispanic American, and Native American) remained stable in D'Youville's population (173 students to 174), another group – reaching 347 – entered the population by 1994. Such a group may have included African Canadians, Caribbean Canadians, etc. who did not identify with United States nomenclature. The students also identified less with Catholicism by 1994; 594 declared themselves non-Catholic and the religion of another 312 is noted as unknown. In the early 1990s, D'Youville had to deal with a strong group of healthcare students. By the late 1990s, graduate education and a growing number of Canadians complicated the social life of the college, as did a far more diverse set of students.[1]

As indicated earlier, Sister Denise initiated the idea of strengthening the healthcare side in the 1980s. Dr. Gertrude Torres, vice president for Academic Affairs (VPAA) had suggested the five-year programs. Torres had also initiated the movement into graduate nursing education. Nurses had a long history at D'Youville – indeed Gery Kopryanski, a D'Youville recruiter, said he argued with the image of D'Youville as a women's nursing college well into the 1990s. The tradition was glorious. By the mid-1990s, the nursing department could count thirty-nine graduates in nursing who had gone on to earn doctorates in some field. In 1988, nurses launched not only into the graduate field (to maintain the field at the college) but also pioneered a program of Friday/Saturday classes that could attract working Canadian nurses with hospital accreditation but in need of the BS and further graduate degrees.

After several VPAAs, Joseph Grande moved up to the position. He was instrumental in getting the physician assistant program through the college (the nursing division with its nurse practitioner

154

Happy smiles continue to be the common feature at hooding ceremonies.

Dr. Jerome Kresse, longtime professor of chemistry at the college hugs his daughter, Mary Ellen, at graduation ceremonies. She was one of five children, all of whom graduated from the college and all of whom have attained graduate degrees and successful careers.

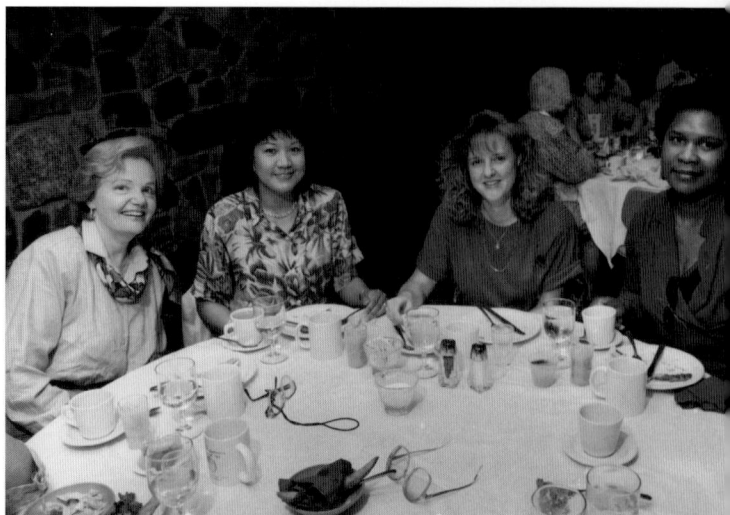

By the 1990s the college had entered graduate education. A group of master's candidates joined together at the traditional alumni brunch in 1991.

program was not pleased). He also initiated the move into Canadian education. Previously, D'Youville had established a program to get Board of Cooperative Educational Services (BOCES) teachers fully accredited. Grande heard from a relative:

> That the University of Toronto had 2,000 applications for 200 positions in their education program . . . So I sent Bob DiSibio [chairperson of education] up to Toronto to the education ministry, provincial ministry, there and I said let them look at our program . . . would they accept it if Canadian students came to us and took our program, because it was much the same as what they did up there . . . There was a minimal amount of change that we had to make in order to make it acceptable to the ministry of education in Ontario. And that's when we began to draw our students from Canada in terms of education. And we drew them. The students were very different than ours. I'll tell you right now. Let's face it, they were shelling out money. Much more than they would have paid if they had gone to Canadian schools. But their attitude was 'we're never going to go unless we do this' and they did . . . What I tried to do before I left office was set up a sequence of courses so that if they came for their certification and if they took just a few more courses they could have a masters.[2]

D'Youville's growth came from identifying niche markets and moving into them strongly, especially when they fit the previous history or inclination (healthcare or education). As Robert Murphy pointed out, answering a question on planning, "I don't think we are overall good planners [but] something has gone right and maybe it's the type of institution that we are that you can't sit there and say I'm going to do this 7-year master plan or whatever the case may be."[3]

While the college expanded in students, the administration, staff, and faculty barely kept up. Administration only grew from sixty-four to sixty-nine individuals, staff from sixty to sixty-nine from

1989 to 1994. Even crucial areas like admissions only grew from seven in 1992 to nine in 1998. The Learning Center was started and maintained with federal grants. When they disappeared, staff was worried about their positions. D'Youville recognized the needs of weaker students who were recruited not only to the "hot" programs, but some of the more traditional areas as well. The college defined helping such students as a critical part of the mission and, indeed, staff in this area grew by one-third from nine to twelve. Even faculty grew only from seventy to eighty-four in the first part of the decade (with an additional twenty-six part-time instructors). In areas like physical therapy and occupational therapy, in some cases the college hired individuals that did not have completed credentials and supported their further education. The college's movement in doctoral programs in health education and educational leadership would meet this need. Faculty in these areas could be extremely overworked. While overload hours in most parts of this faculty were fairly stable in the early 1990s, those in the rehabilitation sciences went from 23 to 114.2. The college's introduction of graduate programs also increased the stress on faculty to do research, even if not directly related to the growth area. Dr. Marion Olivieri who got the first National Science Foundation Grant for D'Youville noted:

Paul Bauer in 1993 when he received the award for outstanding volunteer work in the Buffalo diocese. Part of that work was serving as chairman of the D'Youville Board of Trustees. The college's second major academic building is named in honor of his family.

157

There weren't research facilities, there's not a real sponsored programs office, there's not a huge amount of funding for travel, and stipends for students and all those things . . . They permitted me to go and get things. They did not have to; they could have said no . . .

Verna Kieffer noted a lack of staff, no teaching assistants, yet demands for reaccreditation, writing grants, and establishing new programs.[4]

The divisions within the school also created stress. Elizabeth Stanton, who had a broad background in anthropology and occupational therapy:

I felt that some of the folk believed that we were becoming a cosmetology school, something very vocational. There was then this tension between the traditional academic areas and these professional areas. Then we moved into two schools and that made things even more divided. It was a 'we/they' kind of thing.

The 1999 welcome back faculty picnic on the front lawn of the college.

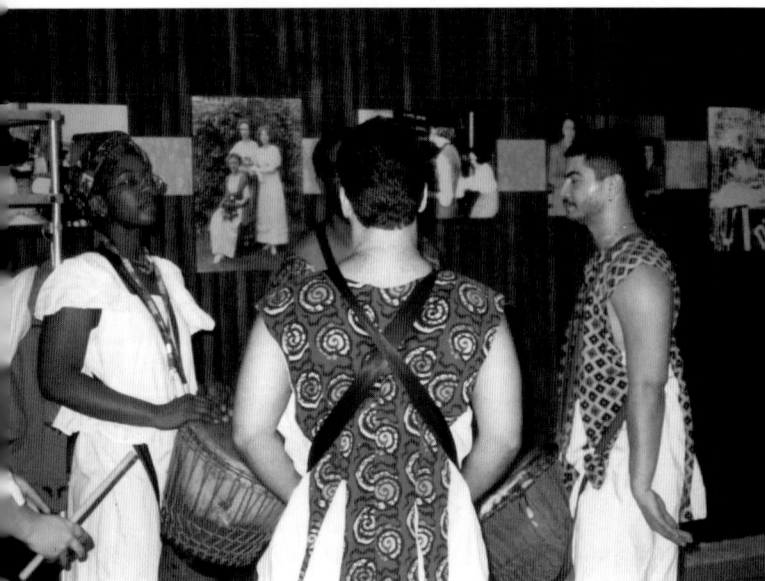

In the 1990s, with diversity at the college growing, new festivals were added to the schedule. In 1996 the African American festival of Kwanzaa was elaborately celebrated.

Later, the influx of Canadian students created questions not so much for faculty but among students. Patricia Polombo who teaches pharmacology, noted:

> I think there's probably more diversity now than there was [she taught years earlier at D'Youville] and that's just absolutely wonderful. And you know there are more Canadians. My graduate nurse practitioner course . . . probably most of the class are Canadians.

However, an education major noted his least favorite memories were of "having to go to school with Canadian students. I [had]... to learn about the Canadian education system, which I have no interest in." While faculty appreciated Canadian students, they also sensed frustration: "It concerns me, as it concerns all of the faculty I've talked to, that U.S. students who are in classes that are predominantly Canadian feel undervalued or excluded, and I don't know how to keep that from happening." A former chairperson of education, Robert Gramble, noted:

> I love our Canadian students – they are excellent students; they are very focused . . . I've got nothing but positive things to say; however, I would like to see in our department an emphasis on American students. We are not sure how long the Canadian population will be there and . . . it's more healthy that we bring in American students.[5]

In student life, the college also experienced divisions. The larger numbers of undergraduates, along with health consciousness among those students and the general population, created a demand for sports programs. In 1996, a men's basketball team once again represented D'Youville. In 1997, plans were laid down to add five additional sports: men and women's golf, men and women's cross country, and women's softball. The last was very successful and the women's team placed third in a national tournament. In 1990, the *D'Youvillian* team pictures show nineteen athletes; by 2000, seventy-nine were shown. Men's baseball and men's volleyball were added, the latter at a championship level. A few years later, 150 athletes played on teams at D'Youville and athletics was recognized as a recruiting tool. Students used a greatly improved training and weight room. The college tore down the old gym (too small by NCAA standards) and rebuilt one of appropriate size. The college also joined the NCAA as a Division III school. Athletics did draw the campus together, to a degree.[6]

CAMPUS MINISTRY remained one of the most active campus associations. In 1992 it had ninety-six students active in Adopt-a-Grandparent, Benedict House, RONALD MCDONALD HOUSE, Skating Association for the Blind and Handicapped (SABAH), and Providence House.

The students in health-related fields demanded athletics – for the good of all they also dominated the Student Government Association (SGA). In 1997, of thirty SGA officers or senators, twenty-six were from these fields; in 1998 and 1999, all but one was from those fields. In the yearbook, the Student Occupational Therapy Association, the Student Physical Therapy Association, and the Student Nurse Associates were almost always pictured. Groups like the history club (Kappa Delta), Artists and Writers, and even the *Catalyst* were pictured or included much less often.[7]

One activity drew from across student groups and included faculty and staff as well. This activity was Competathon. Competathon had rules that teams had to include staff and faculty and commuter as well as dormitory students. The contest ran for a week. It could include scavenger hunts, various games, and smaller contests (several years it included a women's history quiz, since it took place in Women's History Month) and it always ended with several teams in hot contention and virtually no team out of contention. For the finale event, an elaborate air band contest (air bands in the sense of MTV video imitations, lip-synced to popular records). The finale drew two to three hundred folks to the main dining hall for an evening of humor and broad comedy.[8]

Many traditional college activities diminished in the 1990s. The *Catalyst* disappeared for a time in 1995 and thereafter published quarterly at best. After an attempt in the early 1990s to build Moving Up Days into a week-long event (with a leadership dinner, an adult recognition dinner, a signing ceremony for the *Poet*, and a trip to see the Buffalo Bisons play baseball) the MUD concept dwindled. The carnival disappeared in the mid-90s and what remained was a ceremony (the air band from Competathon put on a shortened version of the winning performances), a TGIF, and the semi-formal that was Saturday evening. The sophomore honor society Lambda Sigma remained active through the decade, and other clubs emerged like an ecology club – Earthwise – and at the end of the decade a very active Students in Free Enterprise (SIFE) organization. SIFE organized and included older students but this was rare among clubs. Adult students felt welcomed in class as noted by an employee.

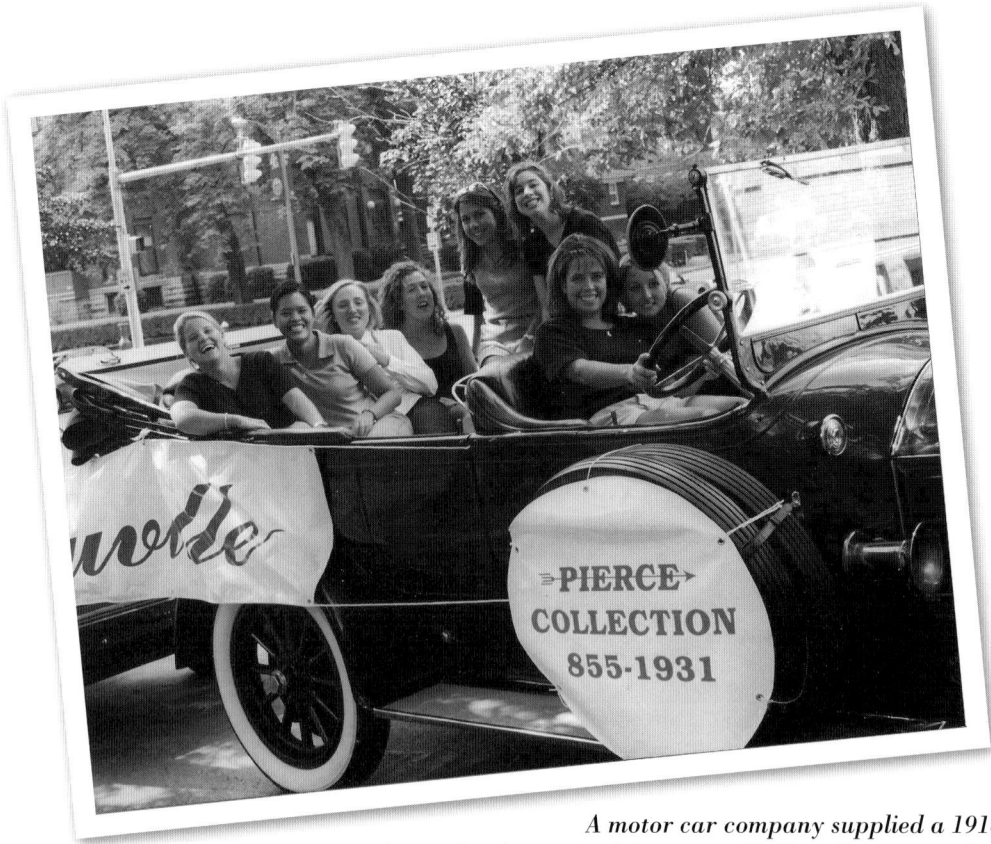

*A motor car company supplied a 1918 Buffalo-made Pierce
Arrow for the 1998 celebration of D'Youville's ninetieth anniversary. The men
and women students took turns driving it at this Welcome Back Picnic on campus.* ────

160

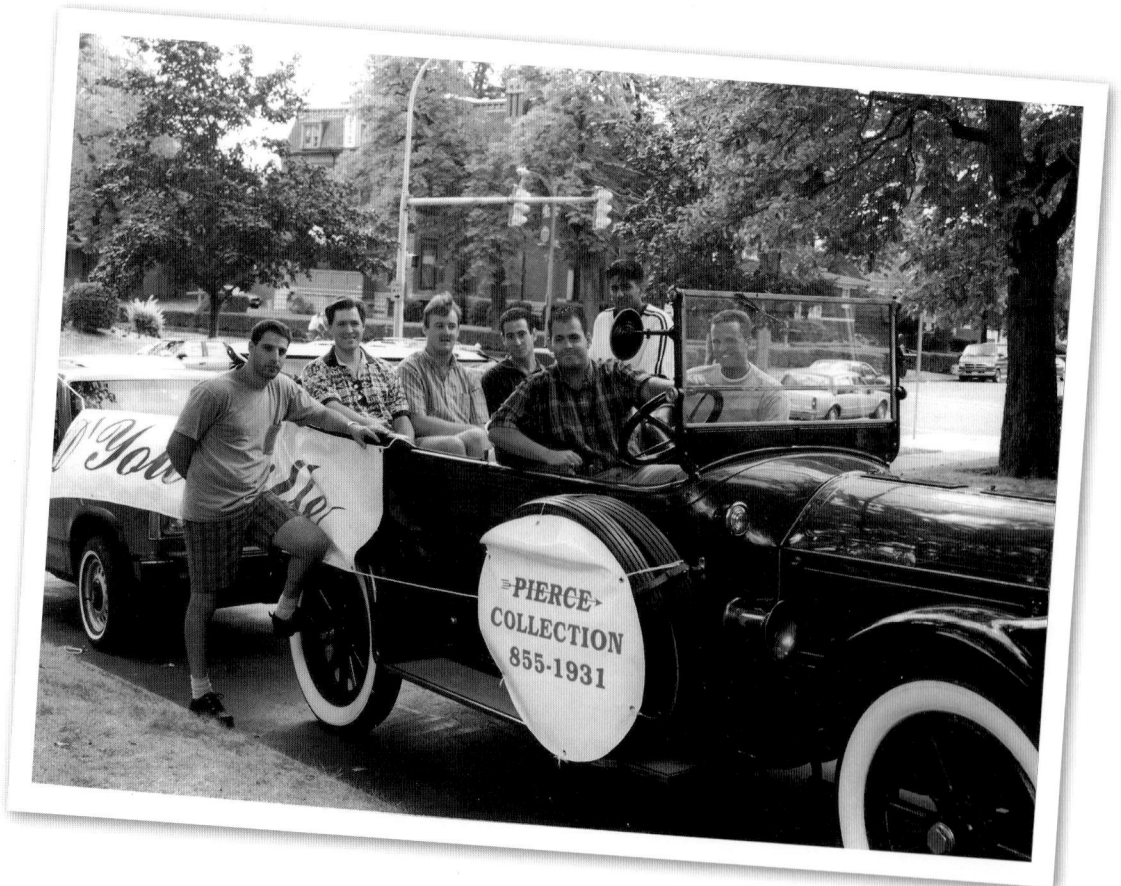

I was in my 40s and it was great going to class; the class mixture was so different. You had adult students, you had the 17-18-year-old students, the 20 year olds, so it was nice, a different aspect of meeting with students and dealing, and I thought it was wonderful. I was a little nervous being out of the classroom for as many years, but the students themselves made me feel comfortable.[9]

Even the traditional attraction to alcohol seemed to have diminished or at least moved off campus. New York State law raised the drinking age to twenty-one which undercut use of alcohol on campus. Earlier, in 1990, the college brought Barry Lillis, a popular weatherman in the area who had abuse problems in the past, as a motivational speaker. In 1990, D'Youville was part of a national survey on drug and alcohol use and in 1991, D'Youville had a Federal Institutions in Post Secondary Education (FIPSE) grant to deal with these issues. A campus survey showed alcohol use less than perceived – almost 40% said D'Youville students drank at least once a week (only 17% did), another third estimated students drank three times a week or more (only 13.4% actually did). Drinking moved off campus.

I had gone to parties, but I wasn't a drinker so if I did go maybe I would have one drink or just bottled water type of thing . . . I never understood the concept of people getting so inebriated that they couldn't walk. It just didn't make sense to me.

Crime statistics showed D'Youville was low in virtually every category except that was mid-range in alcohol-related incidents. Smoking also was barred by New York State law over the decade. Perhaps no alcohol and no tobacco drove partying and dancing off campus. Only live bands like those at the Bellypaloosa festivals could draw in students.[10]

Campus Ministry remained one of the most active campus associations. In 1992 it had ninety-six students active in Adopt-a-Grandparent, Benedict House, Ronald McDonald House, Skating Association for the Blind and Handicapped (SABAH), and Providence House. Later, it urged students

As noted in the text, Hanukkah was also acknowledged. In 1996 the first Menorah joined the Crèche on the front lawn of the college. A local rabbi presides over lighting the first night. ————

into the Crop Walk, Oxfam, Meals on Wheels, Special Olympics, and toy collections for kids at Saint Mary's School for the Deaf. The organization sponsored Building Bridges on disabilities and ecology themes. They also tried to draw the campus together by urging activity with a young adult group in the local parish, and by trying to create a single parent association. They reached out to a more diverse campus continuing to support international luncheons, holding a Seder one year, announcing in the religion column in the *Catalyst* the Jewish High Holy Days, the Muslim Ramadan, and Kwanzaa.[11]

Diversity on campus went beyond Campus Ministry. The BSU and LASO were active throughout the decade. In the late 1990s, an Asian Student Organization joined them. The BSU sponsored a soul food luncheon and a gospel concert to raise funds for its continuing scholarship. Sometimes it arranged a wide range of programs during Black History Month. In September of 1996, LASO offered Latin dance

162

"Oh, there you are." Kwanzaa, 1996.

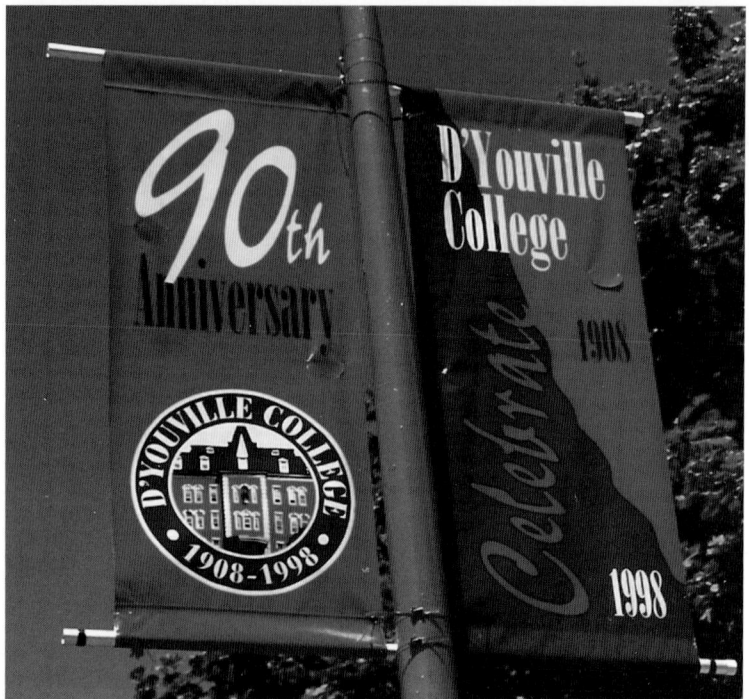

The ninetieth anniversary logo flies before the college.

lessons to the college. In 1996, Yoni Adika organized a Jews on Campus organization. With the support of Campus Ministry, a large Menorah was purchased and lit on the lawn of the college, next to a traditional crèche, a tradition that continues.[12]

As in supporting a Menorah, the college acted to create an office to deal with diversity. In 1993, the Office of Multi-Culturalism was established. The office became a focal point for many minority students on campus. In 1990, the college began to support a trip to Guatemala (later Panama) as a way of building contact and doing service. In 1996, the school issued a statement respecting all religions and banning tests on any religious holiday. Jeff Platt, an administrator, worked to re-establish a commuter council to deal with older students. He also created the Connections Office

Dr. Olga Mendell Karman gives a reading at the 1997 Book Fair.

which served as a service system for all students – need to know how to do something or need a form – go to Connections. But Connections also handled the adult honor society and the adult recognition (OWL – Older Wiser Learner) dinner. The dinner became a stable part of the college calendar.[13]

As an institution, D'Youville supported diversity. The college also supported service. The service was in education to the city of Buffalo. The education department at D'Youville developed an enrichment program with a nearby (one block away) grammar school – renamed the D'Youville Porter Campus School #3. School #3 was 45% Hispanic and 20% African American. The enrichment concentrated on language and mathematics but included sports, summer programs, and health checks. The second project created controversy. In the 1980s, when SUNY at Buffalo declined at the last minute to sponsor a humanities magnet high school – DaVinci – D'Youville offered space. By the 1990s, DaVinci needed more space for four hundred students and additional amenities. When the college provided these by converting two floors of Madonna Hall, a former dormitory, college students protested. The director pointed out the advantage to D'Youville students: expanded computer facilities, opportunity for paid tutor positions, opportunity for educational placement, the fun of mentoring. Eventually the controversy dissipated.[14]

"Sign up here" at the Welcome Back Picnic.

164

"See, there it is."

In the 1990s, growth produced divisions. The college, with its traditions, tried to bridge these gaps. Its history supported diversity and inclusiveness. Religion was always important, but it did not have to be a rigid Catholicism. But sometimes when seeing itself in the Catholic tradition, the administration created controversy. Indeed by the end of the decade there seemed to be a greater emphasis on

Catholicism. As befitting its traditions from 1908, the Catholicism of D'Youville welcomed others, but the issues that caused controversy elsewhere in the 1980s and 1990s surfaced at D'Youville – abortion, availability of condoms, gender segregation in dormitories, the treatment of gays and lesbians. The college's strongest stance on these issues was in relation to abortion. The college promised students they would not in their training be forced to be part of abortion procedures. The administration informally enforced this by refusing placement to institutions where abortion was practiced. This caused controversy among some physician assistant students and some Canadian nurses, but continues to be unwritten policy. The administration never interfered with debate about

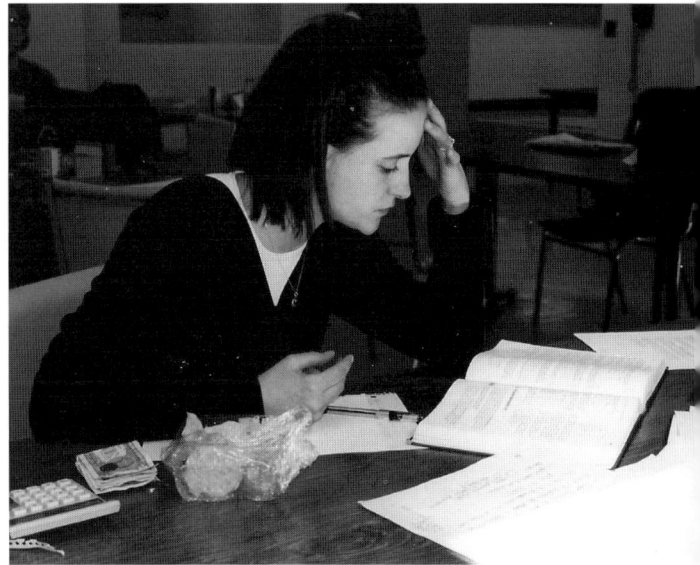

A working lunch.

abortion. Student anti-abortion advocates and pro-choice advocates used the *Catalyst* on several occasions. Professors never felt constrained in the classroom.[15]

The question of gender segregation of living space came in the mid-nineties. The college had only one dorm and until the mid-nineties there were men's floors, women's floors, and one co-ed floor – decided by expediency. The co-ed floor ended in the mid-nineties but in the next decade the college expanded, building an apartment dorm which by its nature is more gender integrated.

The question of supplying condoms on campus is one of sexual activity and the college's refusal to supply condoms was criticized in 1990 and 1994. In regard to the problem of AIDS, the administration was open. There was an official committee to discuss an AIDS policy for the campus. A popular head of Campus Ministry left to head AIDS Family Services and the college provided that organization with office space.[16]

Like the Catholic Church itself, D'Youville never condemned gays or lesbians as people (only sexual practice of gays is questioned). In the late '90s, an article appeared in the *Catalyst* about problems of declaring oneself homosexual. The response was to run a course taught by two acknowledged homosexuals on gays and lesbians in America. Later in the nineties, students organized an Alliance of Gays, Lesbians, Bisexuals, and Transgendered. The alliance applied for student club status and that was granted by the Student Senate. The administration refused. The Vice President for Student Affairs Robert Murphy was brought up before the Judicial Review Board he had organized. Finally, President Sister Denise Roche reached the conclusion that all ideas and interests should be represented and that as long as the club allowed anyone interested in the issues (including heterosexuals) the Alliance would be recognized.[17]

If Catholic traditions remained intact at D'Youville, what of its other traditions of fine teaching, an atmosphere of caring for students, and a warm sympathy like family among faculty and staff? Both Dan Lymans and Tom Milano praised the stimulation they received from the long noted master,

165

Mr. Nielsen. But newer teachers kept up tradition. Nielsen's Socratic ideas found a home in science.

> Am I a teacher? I don't know, you would have to ask my students that, because the only way you would know if I was a teacher [was] I have taught them . . . I don't think really anyone knows whether we actually taught anybody anything. They don't know whether 'they' taught it, or the other person discovered it.

Another of the science faculty came to a similar conclusion:

> But this is a teaching institution and if we want our students to do well we have to be careful that we're not too busy with research . . . You kind of teach these students about learning on their own rather than providing all of the details of everything.

One of the newer faculty in physical therapy adopted this attitude:

> When I first started here I was a professional, I was a physiotherapist, I think I have become more of a professor or an academic. I think that is my primary responsibility and I think it's my best service to my profession. Secondarily, I would be a clinician but I prefer the term teacher. I facilitate learning and critical thinking. I appreciate the term teacher.

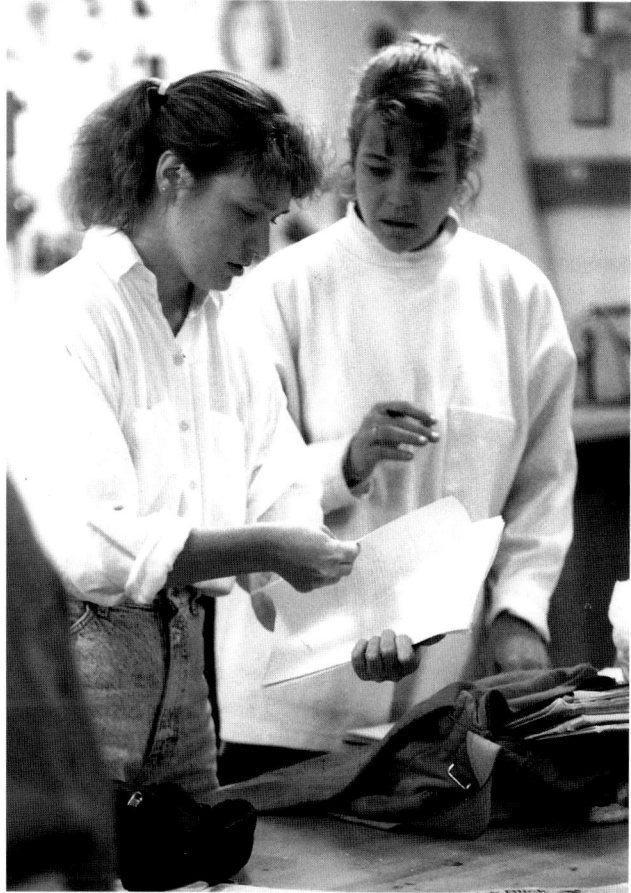

"What!! It's that long?!"

D'YOUVILLE COLLEGE

FIRST WOMEN'S COLLEGE IN WESTERN NEW YORK. ESTABLISHED 1908 BY THE GREY NUNS. CENTER BUILDING, 1874, ORIGINALLY HOUSED HOLY ANGELS ACADEMY. COLLEGE LED RENEWAL OF CITY'S WEST SIDE BY EXPANSION PROGRAM, 1954-1969.

ERIE BICENTENNIAL COMMISSION
BUFFALO & ERIE COUNTY HISTORICAL SOCIETY
1974

The Buffalo and Erie County Historical Society plaque honors D'Youville's history.

167

To honor its hundreds of Canadian students, D'Youville flies both countries' flags. ───────────

Faculty also reflected the joy and the sorrow of the whole teaching procedure.

> It's very satisfying as a faculty person to participate in all the graduation ceremonies, and honor[s] ceremony and I always really enjoy this. When you watch these people start, sometimes as freshmen, and transform themselves, you don't even recognize them after five years and you see them go strolling off. It's really cool.

168

> It was very hard for me at first to have my students graduate, really, really difficult and now I just realize it's sort of like, a time for everything . . . and that that's just the normal sense of things. But it was difficult for me the first couple years to say goodbye to my students . . . [18]

The caring for students is part of good teaching as indicated above, but it also comes through on the student affairs side.

> We love our students, we really do, you're not a number, you have a face, you have a name, most people here know a little bit about you, they can actually have a discussion with you about personal things in your life as opposed to just your grade or the fact that you might be a club officer.

Wardell Mitchell, who handles computer and audio visual equipment, commented:

> No, see it's not the money, it is the money, but I enjoy the work, okay? The money they give me – I'm living off it. But I really enjoy the work. I deal with everybody on campus. Everybody on campus comes through our department. I get motivated by helping people, especially students.

Other employees who started work in the 1990s (as did most of those quoted above) continue to have the family feeling at the college. "If we have any problems we just have to go to certain administrators, instructors or faculty and they will help you out in any way they can. D'Youville has given me and the students just a big family feeling and we are very comfortable here."

Dances make a great break in the routine. Here a couple at the 1998 semi-formal.

Some of that feeling can be very personal and tied to the religious traditions of the college:

> When a student is in need, let's say they don't have the money to continue college. Sister Denise finds a way. I would say the Catholic heritage has never changed here – it's always been here, especially if anyone is ever in need. Sister Denise is highly respected for that reason, that she is here for those that need help . . .

> My mom used to work here and she passed away and we really didn't belong to any church, so Sister Denise not only let us use the chapel, but then she had a huge get-together and everything was free. Our family will never ever be able to repay what she has done for us.[19]

Despite growth, despite emphasis on healthcare professions, and some feeling of division in that, despite growth of graduate programs and the long-term presence of older students, despite the entrance of Canadian students, D'Youville continued its traditions of service, caring, teaching, a place where you grew to know most people and have concern for them, to think of them as a sort of extended family. Why have such strengths continued and will they continue in the new century that began in 2001?

---

[1] *Institutional Self-Study for Commission of Higher Education* by Middle States Association of Colleges and Schools, 1994, p. 59-60. Evaluation file 1990-2000, D'Youville College Archives. Periodic Review Report. Presented by D'Youville College, May 19, 2000, p. 27-29. Evaluation file 2000+, D'Youville College Archives. Interview with Ron Danneker.

[2] Janice Feigenbaum, "History of the Division of Nursing," p. 28-31. Interview with Gary Kopryanski. Interview with Joseph Grande.

[3] Interview with Robert Murphy.

[4] Institutional Self Study . . . 1994, p. 36, p. 68. *D'Youvillian*, 1992, 1998. Interviews with Theresa Vallone, Elizabeth Stanton, Verna Kieffer, John Rousselle, Joseph Grande, Marion Olivieri, Lynn Rivers, Mary Ellen Moriarty.

[5] Interviews with Elizabeth Stanton, Sean Sullivan, Patricia Polumbo, Sister Nancy Kaczmarek, Robert Gamble.

[6] *D'Youvillian*, 1990-2000. Catalyst, (October 1996) p. 13; (November 1996); 23:8 (May 1997).

[7] Catalyst, 23:5 (February 14, 1997) p. 6; 25:7 (April 1998) p. 1; 27:4 (May 1999) p. 1. *D'Youvillian*, 1990-2000 (1999 was not published for lack of interest.)

[8] Interviews with James DeHaven, Elizabeth Stanton, Theresa Vallone. *Catalyst*, (February 29, 1996).

[9] *D'Youvillian*, 1990-2000. Interview with Carol Milazzo.

[10] Catalyst (November 1990); (October 1993); 23:6 (February 1999) on smoking (February 14, 1990); 23:6 (April 1997). *D'Youvillian*, 1990. Institutional Self Study . . . 1994, p. 105, D'Youville College Archive. Interview with Tom Milano.

[11] Catalyst (February 5, 1990) p. 1; (January 1991); (November 1992); (October 1993); (October 1996); 23:6 (April 1997); (Summer 1997); 23:4 (December 1996); 24:1 (September 1997) p. 7; 23:5 (February 1997).

[12] *D'Youvillian*, 1990-2000; *Catalyst*, (February 9, 1996); (September 1996); 23:4 (December 1996).

[13] *Catalyst*, (December 1990); (September 1993); (February 1996) p. 7. (April 22, 1996) p. 11; Email Robert Murphy, D'Youville Oral History Project.

[14] Robert DiSibio and Robert Gamble. "Collaboration Between Schools and Higher Education." *College Student Journal*, 31:4 (December 1997). *Catalyst*, (November 1990) p. 15; (April 1991); (February 1992).

[15] Interview with Debra Owens. Interview with Elizabeth Stanton. *Catalyst*, (March 21, 1990); (May 7, 1990); (December 1990); (March 1994).

[16] Interview with Deborah Owens. *Catalyst*, (February 14, 1990) p. 6; (April 1994).

[17] Estenek, Sandra, "A Study of Student Affairs Practices at Catholic Colleges and Universities," *Current Issues in Catholic Education* (Winter 1996) p. 63-72. Interview with Robert Murphy. *Catalyst* 24:2 (October 1997); 24:3 (November 1997); 27:2 (March 12, 1999); 27:3 (April 1999).

[18] Interviews with James DeHaven, Marian Olivieri, Eric Miller, Andrew Schmitz, M. Ruth Kelly.

[19] Interviews with Deborah Owens, Wardell Mitchell, Annie Walters, Cheryl Saramak.

Chapter Ten

Growth Toward What?

In 1936, Harvard University celebrated its three hundred-year anniversary. The university was small—fewer than five thousand—its fame rested on longevity, a successful switch to the German University model of education at the turn of the century, and distinguished alumni. The rather stodgy faculty debated whether to invite its most noted graduate, President Franklin Roosevelt, to speak (he had only been a gentleman "C" student and his politics were viewed as abominable) and how to handle German universities since they were officially part of the reprehensible Nazi State in Germany (Roosevelt did speak and individual German scholars were invited to the ceremonies). Harvard was the leading university but it feared rivals like University of Chicago, Johns Hopkins, Stanford, Yale, and Michigan. Most of those institutions were also small. No one had billion dollar endowments, vast research connections to the federal government, or students with uniform high academic motivation. The institution that is Harvard today, lay in the future (really after the 1950s) for the school.[1]

Certainly, its distinguished alumni record and the earlier choice of being a research university shaped

172

A variety of students march in for hooding in the baccalaureate service in 2002.

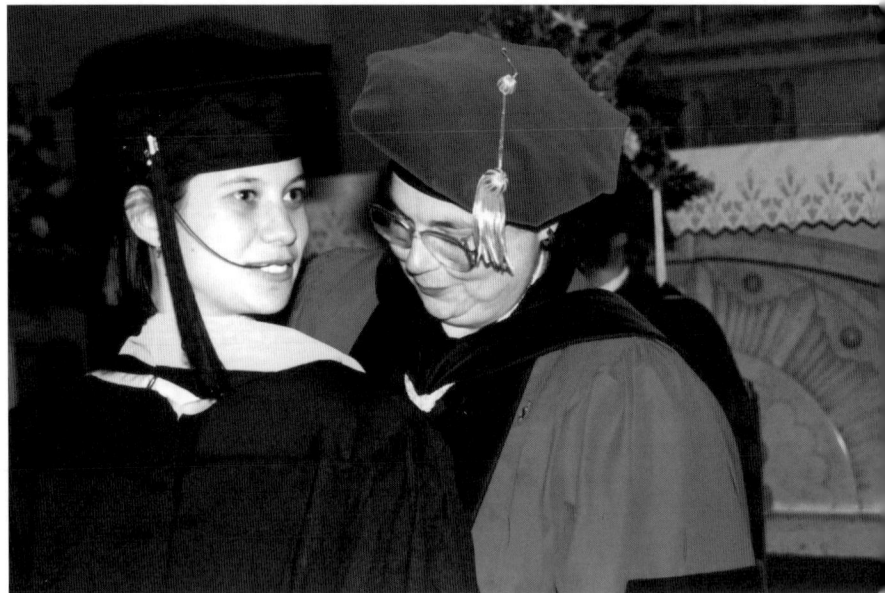

Dr. Janet Ihlenfeld hooding a student. A graduate of the college returned as a faculty member, she was well loved by her nursing students despite an on-line practice video game which left them trapped in the bathroom if they forgot to virtually wash their hands. She died suddenly and unexpectedly in the middle of her career.

its future, but in 1936 the vision of Harvard of today was not clear. In the first decade of the twenty-first century, D'Youville College reached its one hundredth anniversary. Like Harvard, its future is not entirely clear. Also of question is how the past will shape the future of the college. The current administration of Sister Denise Roche has created stability and tremendous growth. For the first time since the late '50s and early '60s, there is a vision of an actual campus and buildings to create it. In 1998, the old Holy Angels Grammar School was purchased, gutted, and rebuilt into a new library. The great dome skylight of Our Lady was uncovered and restored (it had been sealed

> **THE FUTURE OF THE COLLEGE** lies then in its past – a continued mix of healthcare and education – focused primarily on professional development, but not necessarily **THE TRADITIONAL PROFESSIONAL TRIO** of doctor, lawyer, university professor.

off when the building was rented to the public school system). Next, in 2001, the old library (built in the 1950s) was torn out and a new academic building that connected the original buildings to the Health Science Building (now named Alt for Pauline Alt, a distinguished alumna) was erected. At the other end of the complex, Madonna Hall was transformed into classrooms for the expansion of DaVinci High School (a public high school that began on the campus in 1988). Later, in 2002, the gym connected to the college center was torn down and a new expanded gymnasium (to meet most NCAA Division III requirements) was erected in the same place. The college then purchased two blocks of houses north of the campus, on Connecticut Avenue, to erect a new apartment dormitory in 2003 and extended parking facilities. They also purchased the block of houses east of West Avenue for more parking. The campus now surrounds Holy Angels Parish Church instead of being an off-shoot from that institution. The last step of the plan is to build another large academic building where once the old laundry stood, on current parking lots. This largest, closest parking will become green space and Fargo Avenue (dividing the campus) will be partly closed and partly used as an entrance to the college. D'Youville will have a campus.

What justifies all this building is the continued expansion of the college enrollment. Total numbers rose from just under one thousand undergraduates and thirteen hundred graduates in 1999, to eight hundred undergraduates and two thousand graduates in 2003. The growth of graduate students, as noted in the last chapter, was from Canadian education majors. The growth has continued with the latest number at a bit over three thousand, but with a slightly better mix of undergraduate to graduate students. New programs, like chiropractic, blend undergraduate and professional degrees. The projected building will primarily house a School of Pharmacy, extending the healthcare focus. As in the rest of the country, nursing enrollment (mainly undergraduate) has also returned to earlier large numbers. While Sister Denise has stated a need to return to a majority of undergraduates (they are more stable in that they are at D'Youville longer), she has recognized the growth of graduate education to the extent of looking for new programs, creating doctoral level degrees, and seeking university status. She does not envision more than a few hundred new students to a population of thirty-five hundred to four thousand.[2]

The future of the college lies then in its past – a continued mix of healthcare and education – focused primarily on professional development, but not necessarily the traditional professional trio of doctor,

173

Demolition of the 1956 library in 2000. A new library was in place. Eventually this space was filled with the Bauer Family Academic Center.

lawyer, university professor. The college does have alumni in all those areas and in other prominent positions as well. Some of the prominent alumni have already been mentioned, like Ann Wood the aviator from World War II who continued flying and retired as an executive vice-president at Pan American Airlines and Sister Rosalie Bertell, the cancer specialist. Others have appeared in these pages as both alumni and faculty or staff members. These members of the college community received their BA or BS degrees from the college and went on to higher degrees or the PhD, these include Dorothy M. Bellanti, Sister Mary Brendan Connors, Margaret Curry, Sister Mary Kathleen Duggan, Maureen Finney, Paul Hageman, Janet Ihlenfeld, Sister Nancy Kaczmarek, M. Ruth Kelly, Canio Marasco, Sister Joan Maureen McInerney, Tom Milano, Pamela Miller, Mary Ellen Moriarty, Marian Olivieri, Karen Piotrowski, Sister Denise Roche, Judith Schiffert, Judith Stanley, Theresa Vallone, and Patricia Van Dyke.

Through the decades others have reached renown. From 1930 was Julia Mahoney. She was a student of Elizabeth Cronyn, the D'Youville voice teacher who made her own debut at Milan's La Scala. After completing her work at D'Youville, Julia studied at the graduate school of the Julliard in New York City. In the early 1930s, she won the Columbia Broadcasting System's national audition contest and became leading soloist on their coast to coast program with Andre Kostelanetz and his orchestra. She sang in Washington for President and Mrs. Hoover. When her mother became ill, she returned to Buffalo and soon began what became a dedication of thirty years, teaching in the Community Music School of Buffalo. In 1978 the school recognized her devotion by naming her Master Teacher. In 1946 Jean Ripton Peterson graduated magna cum laude in history. She took her law degree at Cornell University, with distinction, ranking first in the entire law school. Admitted to the bar in 1949, she married Bertil Peterson, Esquire. Determined to continue her career in law as she raised her family of six sons and two daughters, Jean became one of the nine legal assistants to the New York State Board of Examiners, a position she held for twenty-seven years. She was also counsel to the Erie County Court, town supervisor in Hamburg, and Hamburg town attorney. Over the years, she has served as an officer of the Erie County Bar Association and as president of the Women Lawyers of Western New York. Edith Flanigen graduated in 1950 with a bachelor's degree in chemistry (magna cum laude). She became an industrial chemist and attained international prominence for her work in the fields of silicate chemistry and the chemistry of zeolites and molecular sieve materials. She invented, for instance, the hydrothermal emerald synthesis process. She has authored or co-authored 36 publications and has been granted 104 U.S. patents. Dr. Marilyn Repsher, '52, who took her doctorate at Columbia University, was nationally recognized as the University and College Professor of the Year, 1999-2000, for her outstandingly successful work with students of mathematics at Jacksonville University in Jacksonville, Florida.

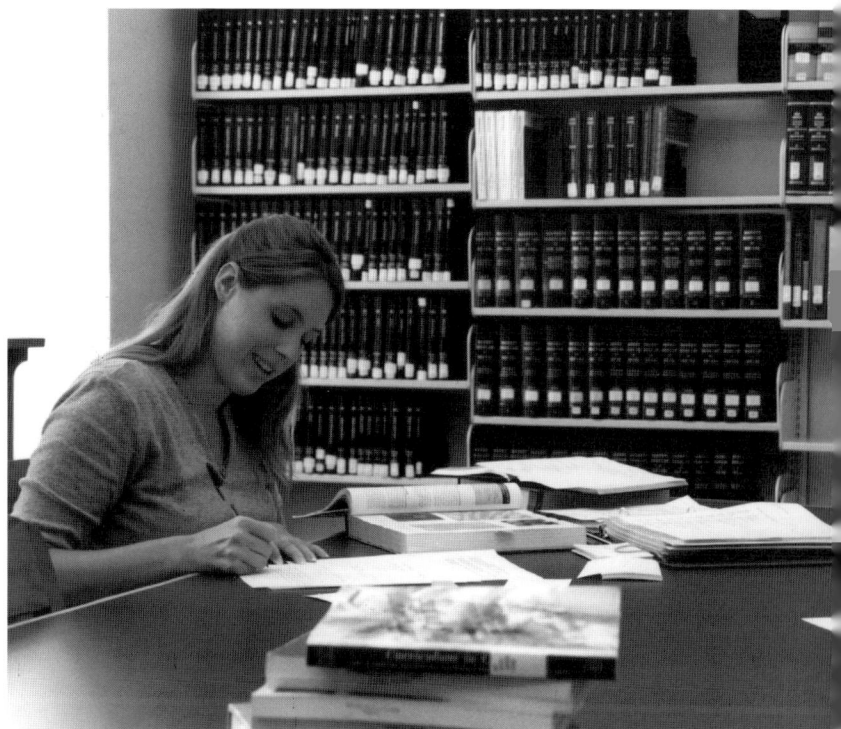

Student at work in the new library, the restored Holy Angels Elementary School.

175

Patricia O'Mara Rehak, '62, was for fourteen years a moving spirit at the Buffalo-Niagara Partnership and its predecessor the Greater Buffalo Development Foundation. When she retired because of ill health in 2002, she was the executive vice-president of the Partnership, working closely with Andrew J. Rudnick, president. She was the face behind the formation of the Buffalo Niagara Enterprise regional marketing campaign which drew together private sector investors and launched a $5 million-a-year regional marketing campaign. Also in 1962 Marcella Farinelli (later, Fierro) took her BS in biology. She has been cited here lauding Sister Margaret of the Sacred Heart, Sister Mary Sheila, Sister Catherine of Siena, and Sister Marie Christine. "Mr. Grande was the new history prof, and Dr. Antanas Musteikis taught the best soc class ever. Dr. Donald Po-Chedley was my biology teacher.... It was he and Sister Mary Josephine who didn't think it was weird for me to want to go to medical school when the rest of the world thought that, including the medical school." She became the chief medical examiner of the Commonwealth of Virginia in 1994. Fierro has also taught legal medicine and pathology at the Medical College of Virginia, the University of Virginia in Charlottesville, and the East Carolina School of Medicine in Greenville. She has also served as a consultant to the FBI's Task Force on National Crime. She has lectured extensively and been published in numerous peer review journals. She has also appeared on the Discovery Channel's *New Detective* series and on BBC. The May 2005 issue of *National Geographic* featured Marcella in the article, "The Poison Paradox." Patricia Cornwell, the very successful mystery novelist, has said that the idea for her lead character, Kay Scarpetta, would never have occurred to her had she not met Fierro in 1984.

THE SKYLIGHT uncovered in the restoration work for the new library in 1999. It remains a feature of the fourth floor.

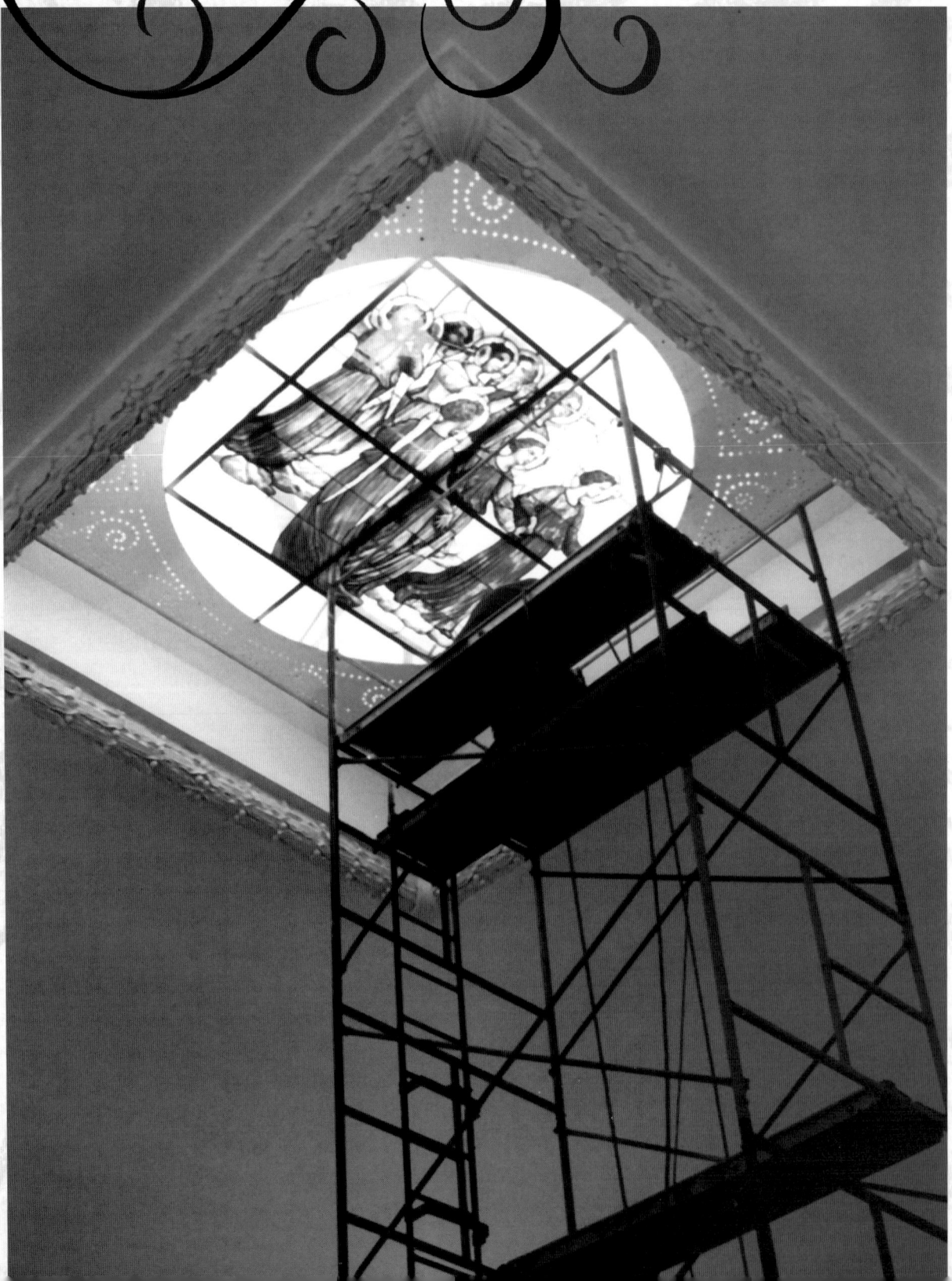

Three notable graduates were produced in 1965. Dr. Marilyn Mahoney Fleckenstein, professor of philosophy and director of the Learn and Serve Program at Niagara University, recently has been named associate vice president for Academic Affairs there. In New York City, Bonne Tymorski Mogulescu recently assumed the position of provost and vice president for Academic Affairs at NYC College of Technology. Linda Yarr took her BA in French when she graduated in 1965. Her French stood her in good stead when, after completing a master's in government and Southeast Asia studies at Cornell, she went on to Paris, France, for an advanced degree in international relations. After serving as a member of the first U.S. civilian delegation to Vietnam in 1986, working on the educational system, Linda became the executive director of the George Washington University Program for International Studies in Asia. This organization enlists leaders from China, Vietnam, Laos, Malaysia, and Mongolia in efforts to secure peace and economic growth in the twenty-first century. Linda designs development courses. In collaboration with the China Foreign Affairs University in Beijing, she helps improve the teaching of international negotiations, crisis management, and public diplomacy. Another alumna eminent in the field of law was class of '66 graduate, Mary E. Bisantz, who, after many distinguished years of service as an administrative law judge in the Office of Hearings and Appeals in Raleigh, North Carolina, retired in 2007 as the Honorable Mary E. Bisantz, deputy chief judge of the Social Security Disability Program. Finally from 1977, is Marsal Naples Stoll who, since 1999 had been vice president for Instruction and Student Services at Piedmont Community College in Charlottesville, Virginia, and who has been appointed the new president of Houston Community College's Coleman College of Health Sciences, located in the Texas Medical Center, the largest medical center in the world.

177

The college also has hundreds of alumni who are primary and secondary schoolteachers, nurses, occupational therapists, physical therapists, physician assistants, medical administrators, mid-level business managers, and formerly social workers and medical technicians. Since its first decade, when D'Youville created a program to upgrade those already teaching, D'Youville has tried to service special groups in professional development. Across America, if you are unfortunate enough to end up at a

Students enjoying the space of the new library in 2001.

View of the apartment style dorm completed in 2005, the first campus expansion north of Connecticut Avenue.

hospital, the name D'Youville is likely to be recognized. No one can work in the local school systems without colleagues that are D'Youville alumni. These alumni overwhelmingly feel their D'Youville education fully prepared them for their positions, brought them a full knowledge of their individual field, and helped them relate that field to broader societal and world concerns. Many feel prepared to become leaders in their local institutions.

The past will also shape the future of the college in four other areas – strongly or weakly is yet to be seen. These areas are a rich sense of caring for the students, and a virtual family sense among particularly the staff (hence the title of this book). Related to those caring attitudes is a deep call to focus on teaching, and finally, related to all is the college focus on religion and particularly Catholicism. All four of these areas are currently interrelated and all are strongly rooted in the history of this college.

Alumni from the 1920s to the 1990s note that D'Youville was an intimate, caring institution. In the early days when sisters and students lived in the same building and when sisters did the majority of the teaching, the sense of caring flowed clearly from the sisters to their female charges. All those dedications in the early yearbooks to the sisters indicate this. Students learned also to care for

Left to right: Chairman
of the Board Kevin Dillon,
Buffalo Mayor Anthony
Masiello, and D'Youville
President Sister Denise
Roche are all smiles at
the dorm's dedication
in 2005.

179

Student assistants
at the Centennial
Kickoff Party,
December 2007,
dress in the costumes
of various decades.

At the Centennial Kickoff Party, the Honorable Stephen Brereton, consul general from the Canadian Consulate in Buffalo and a trustee of D'Youville, presents a well known Inuit sculpture called an Inukshuka on behalf of the people of Canada to Sister Denise Roche, president of the college.

180

each other. Alumni have life-long bonds that show up in fall alumni reunions. (All colleges provide this, but not perhaps to the same extent.) If the caring attitude started among the sisters, it has continued among faculty, staff, and administration. Sister Denise is particularly known for finding a way as a last-ditch-effort among students. Every year she tells the graduating class at the alumni breakfast that she and the Grey Nuns will always pray for them, that D'Youville is where they can always come home. The caring attitude, however, goes beyond the sisters and extends over time. Every year the students vote a staff, administrator, and a faculty award. The staff and administrator awards have often gone to the folks in student activities, but it has also gone to the woman who insists they pay their bills. In 1970, the *D'Youvillian* was dedicated to Dolores Sullivan as she retired as the college nurse. In the 1980s Robert Nielsen was the dedicatee – he had served and would continue to serve as an informal counselor, not only to students, but to faculty and staff as well.[3] Taking care of students as indicated in previous pages, is part of the culture of the Student Life staff. It is also part of faculty culture. Senior colleagues watch and judge junior colleagues' interactions with students. Faculty discuss (perhaps with slight

A drummer and the centennial banner precede the faculty procession to the one hundredth baccalaureate service and hooding.

violation of student rights) how students are doing, to check whether there is a general or a particular problem. As noted in text, students do feel free to talk with faculty.

Closely related to the atmosphere of caring is the idea that D'Youville College is a second family. This was noted and presented in these pages primarily from folks on the staff. While D'Youville does not pay the best wages in Buffalo, it is a good place to work. Staff value (and it is a tremendous financial benefit) the right to send their children to college at no cost. But the family feeling flows more directly

SISTER DENISE reads the citation as Bishop Edward Kmiec, bishop of Buffalo, is hooded as a **DOCTOR OF HUMANE LETTERS** at the 2008 baccalaureate and hooding service.

from pro-family rules on maternity and health leaves (some of this is done informally with faculty, staff, and administrators just filling in for each other), with the rules allowing some flexibility in schedule to meet family needs, etc. This attitude comes through in times of crisis as when Sister Denise offered college facilities for a funeral service, or times when she has approached the family of staff, faculty, or administrators when trouble with the law, sickness, or death has occurred. Everyone knows the president will be there for them to the extent she can without affecting the reputation of the college. The family feeling, obviously, is related to the notion of caring about one another and also about the students.

What makes for great teaching? First, caring about the students; second, exhibiting a great passion for what you are teaching. From these pages, listed from the start of the college are lay instructors. They include in the first thirty or forty years, Miss Cronin, a world recognized singer, who showed her students style and flair and brought famous performers to do campus concerts; Dr. Lappin whose scholarship and contacts brought outstanding speakers to the campus. They were joined in the 1920s and 1930s by Sister Saint Ignatius who inspired brilliant work from her students in history, and Father Healy who was known as the labor priest in Buffalo and helped round out the social work program. In the 1950s and 1960s, they were joined by Father Beechler who shocked many students with his views on theology; Joe Grande, passionate about history; and Donald PoChedley whose research and teaching inspired biology students. Sister Virginia Carley and Kevin Cahill were deeply remembered by all students, not just in English. During the wild days of the 1960s and 1970s, Dr. Antanas Musteikis with his great dignity and warmth, helped keep the lid on while Mr. Nielsen became the wise counselor to many and the one to stir up questions as he taught philosophy. While this list, drawn from interviews, seems to favor the liberal arts, others were also remembered. Sister Francis Xavier in nursing; Joseph Fennell in business; Ruth Sietz, Jamie DeWaters, and Sister Joan Maureen McInerney in education. The faculty award mentioned earlier voted by the seniors, is felt by the faculty to be the finest distinction. Faculty in all areas have been recognized, including in the sciences and in the new professional fields like physical therapy.

While the classroom, laboratory, clinical, and office settings are where these teachers transmit their learning and attitudes to the student, the second part of great teaching is the passion for the subject. This passion finds expression in teaching wide varieties of courses, doing research and scholarship, and simply remaining abreast of one's field. The faculty doesn't generally see a distinction between scholarship and teaching, but puts greater emphasis on teaching. Time constraints and limits are certainly part of this.

Caring, a family attitude, and fine teaching are all shaped at D'Youville by its Catholic traditions and continued religious orientation. The Catholicism of D'Youville College has always been subtle. Holy Angels Academy from which it grew had included Protestants and at both the academy and the college there were exemptions from religious classes for Protestants. However, from the origins to the 1950s, few non-Catholics attended. (There was one notable Lutheran minister's daughter in 1930s.) The young women of the early years felt they were symbols for the superiority of their college and their faith. In the early years, Professor Lappin considered himself a Catholic scholar (he rejected Joyce as

184

A stirring ecumenical service in Holy Angels Church opened the centennial year on January 30, 2008. This shot of faculty and choir focuses on the brilliant rose window.

anti-Catholic while recognizing the quality of his writing). The young women were proud their college included spirituality as well as science and the liberal arts. They rejected any notion of secularization as an incomplete education. (These debates were alive in higher education in the 1940s and 1950s.) However, Professor Grande who came in the 1950s to teach history, never felt any constraints as to what he brought to the classroom – and this also seemed part of the tradition.

Part of these early traditions was a philosophy of service. Virtually from the first year, the young women of D'Youville sponsored Christmas parties and gifts for the Father Baker homes and for a poor parish on the north side of Buffalo. Later this activity shifted to Saint Mary's School for the Deaf. Social life, in part, revolved around the Sodality of Mary. During World War I, alumnae served in France as nurses and care workers. Of course during World War II, there were blood drives and other types of social service as well as graduating nurses entering the Army Nurse Corps and the WAVES.

Until the 1950s, American Catholicism was distinctly a minority religion. With the rise of anti-communism (long a church position) and certainly the election of President Kennedy in 1960, American Catholicism entered the American mainstream. In the early 1970s, when the Catholic Church adopted Vatican II reforms, what it meant to be Catholic shifted. The Catholic Church began to see itself as part of the broader ecumenical Christianity (albeit as first and leader). This shift along with the upsurge of social activism in society meant that Catholicism became more open at D'Youville. As male Catholic colleges opened their doors to women, the college became more diverse in programs, and admitted men, etc. to meet the growing competition.

By the 1960s, *Mary's Mantle* (the paper of Sodality) had yielded to more secular journalistic effort like campus newspaper, *The Disc*. Sodality evolved into Campus Ministry, which was to remain a major campus organization to the present. Campus Ministry stressed service to the community and an ecumenical faith approach – Protestants, Jews, Muslims were all welcomed and supported. The service idea spread across many organizations. The Student Council for Exceptional Children did highly supported dance marathons in the '60s and '70s.

At this one hundredth commencement, the graduating class has grown from its initial 5 to 750. —————————————

188

Sister Elizabeth Bagen, vice president of the Grey Nuns of the Sacred Heart, reads the citation honoring ninety-six-year-old Sister Alice for her fifty-four years of service to D'Youville, 1942–1996, thirty-two years of which were as Registrar. The Registrar's Office is hereafter known as the Sister Alice McCollester Office.

At the April 2008 Employees Recognition Dinner, Sister Denise, right, honors Sister Mary Charlotte Barton, left, former president of the college, and Sister Marlene Butler, president of the Grey Nuns and a former dean of students at D'Youville.

The Student Nursing Association has done blood drives for decades. The Black Student Union has raised scholarship money since its inception in the '70s. All clubs are currently requested to do some social service every year.

Social service, as noted here, is a major part of the Catholic and perhaps more particularly the Grey Nuns' heritage. But in another sense the entire focus of the college is devoted to the service of society. Instructors teach students who enter primarily service professions, in education, healthcare, and ethical business practice. A good proportion of these students come from less advantaged educational backgrounds and it is a service to give them the skills to succeed in modern society. The Learning Center, still headed by a Grey Nun, Sister Mary Brendan, is integral to this aspect of the college.

D'Youville will never again be an institution where the majority of faculty and staff are nuns and priests. It may at some point even have a lay president. But its mission shaped the attitude of caring for others – caring for students and the D'Youville family, the care and concern that makes the focus on teaching. These aspects should never be lost, regardless of future growth or prestige.

---

[1] Morton and Phyllis Keller. *Making Harvard Modern.* New York: Oxford, (2001) p. 3-10.

[2] D'Youville College Self Study, presented to the Middle States Commission on Higher Education, (April 2005) p. 44. Comments by Sister Denise Roche, (January 31, 2008).

[3] *D'Youvillian,* 1980 and 1990.

189